Elite • 247

Roman Plate Armour

M.C. BISHOP

ILLUSTRATED BY GIUSEPPE RAVA
Series editors Martin Windrow & Nick Reynolds

OSPREY PUBLISHING
Bloomsbury Publishing Plc
Kemp House, Chawley Park, Cumnor Hill, Oxford OX2 9PH, UK
29 Earlsfort Terrace, Dublin 2, Ireland
1385 Broadway, 5th Floor, New York, NY 10018, USA
E-mail: info@ospreypublishing.com
www.ospreypublishing.com

OSPREY is a trademark of Osprey Publishing Ltd

First published in Great Britain in 2022

© Osprey Publishing Ltd, 2022

All rights reserved. No part of this publication may be reproduced or
transmitted in any form or by any means, electronic or mechanical,
including photocopying, recording, or any information storage or retrieval
system, without prior permission in writing from the publishers.

A catalogue record for this book is available from the British Library.

ISBN: PB 9781472851871; eBook 9781472851864;
ePDF 9781472851840; XML 9781472851857

22 23 24 25 26   10 9 8 7 6 5 4 3 2 1

Index by Rob Munro
Typeset by PDQ Digital Media Solutions, Bungay, UK
Printed and bound in India by Replika Press Private Ltd.

Osprey Publishing supports the Woodland Trust, the UK's leading woodland
conservation charity.

To find out more about our authors and books visit
www.ospreypublishing.com. Here you will find extracts, author
interviews, details of forthcoming events and the option to sign up for
our newsletter.

Acknowledgements

I am grateful to Dr Christian Miks of the Römisch-Germanisches
Zentralmuseum for his help in obtaining the photograph of the Numantia
pectorale. Dr Stefan Burmeister of Varusschlacht im Osnabrücker Land
GmbH once again helped with illustrations, including some from the recent
new find from Kalkriese. Pascal Lemaire very kindly allowed me to include
his image of the Carlisle backplate. Dr Arik Greenberg was good enough to
supply images of his reconstructions, while Drs Fraser Hunter, Holger von
Grawert and Ross Cowan also helped with the sourcing of images. As ever,
my friend and colleague Dr Jon Coulston allowed me to dip into his vast
collection of images, for which I thank him, almost as much as for agreeing
to read and comment upon an early draft of this text. I am also grateful to
Mariel Hennequin of the Musée Jeanne d'Aboville for images of and
information about the Versigny figurine. Last, but most definitely not least,
thanks are also due to Dr Frances McIntosh of English Heritage's Corbridge
Roman Site and Museum for arranging for some of the Corbridge Hoard
armour to be examined with a pXRF machine to confirm a long-harboured
suspicion of mine.

Artist's note

Readers may care to note that the original paintings from which the colour
plates in this book were prepared are available for private sale. All
reproduction copyright whatsoever is retained by the publishers. All
enquiries should be addressed to:

info@g-rava.it

The publishers regret that they can enter into no correspondence upon
this matter.

Title-page photograph: Detail of *lorica segmentata* fittings depicted on
Trajan's Column. From a cast in the Museo della Civiltà Romana. (Photo
© M.C. Bishop)

Back cover, middle: Reconstructed cuirass in the Museo della Civiltà
Romana in Rome using Groller's reconstruction to interpret the *lorica
segmentata* finds from Carnuntum. (Photo © M.C. Bishop)

CONTENTS

ROMAN PLATE ARMOUR

INTRODUCTION

Roman plate armour is one of the most easily recognizable cultural identifiers of any of the peoples in the ancient world. Whether it be the ubiquitous *lorica segmentata* of the ordinary troops, or the muscled cuirasses of senior officers, the modern observer obediently follows an iconographic agenda set nearly 2,000 years ago on a monument in the centre of Trajan's Forum in Rome.

Trajan's Column was constructed using the not inconsiderable proceeds of the Emperor Trajan's (r. AD 98–117) two wars of AD 101–02 and AD 105–06 in Dacia (closely approximating to modern Romania) and completed in AD 113. Its inscription merely highlighted the fact that it marked the depth of the excavations undertaken to complete Trajan's Forum, but the sculpted helical frieze running anti-clockwise up its shaft left no doubt that its real purpose was to commemorate and glorify Trajan's trans-Danubian conquests. Although it was long thought that 'field sketches' may have been used as visual aids, it is now believed that the metropolitan sculptors made reference to what they saw around them in Rome, where they would of course have been familiar with the sight of troops, whether they were the Praetorian Guard, the *equites singulares Augusti*, or passing bodies of provincial legionaries and auxiliaries. It is as well to remember, however, that just because they could observe armour, it did not necessarily mean that they understood what they were seeing.

In order to make its visual message simple to onlookers (who could not only view it from ground level but also from surrounding galleries in the forum), types of troops in the opposing armies were stereotyped into particular groups. Roman citizen troops (both legionaries and Praetorians) were depicted wearing articulated plate cuirasses (the famed *lorica segmentata*), while most non-citizen auxiliary troops wore mail to distinguish them from their social superiors. Senior officers, usually Trajan himself and his accompanying advisors, were shown wearing Hellenistic-style muscled cuirasses, probably made of metal plate (see p.49 for a discussion of the material used). Inevitably, because large numbers of citizen troops are shown on the frieze, *lorica segmentata* has seeped into the Western cultural perception of what a Roman soldier looked like, assisted by works such as those of Piranesi or Just Lips (aka Iustus Lipsius) that referenced Trajan's Column. This was undoubtedly helped by the willingness of medieval and early modern artists, followed by Hollywood, to adopt the convenient visual shorthand it offered when producing Roman 'sword and sandal' epics.

Citizen soldiers depicted on Trajan's Column working in their *lorica segmentata*. From a cast in the Museo della Civiltà Romana. (Photo © M.C. Bishop)

The prominence of the Trajan's Column reliefs is in many ways enhanced by the comparative rarity of depictions of *lorica segmentata* in provincial art. It may be glimpsed in one or two places, such as one of the pedestal reliefs from the legionary headquarters building in Mainz (Germany) or, possibly, on a relief from Saintes (France), but it is surprisingly absent from the canon of tombstone reliefs from the 1st century AD. The bulk of the surviving representations are on metropolitan sculpture from the city of Rome itself, wholly or partly influenced by the helical frieze of Trajan's Column. Some slightly earlier, large-scale reliefs believed to be from the Temple of the Gens Flavia on the Quirinal Hill in Rome include a soldier wearing *segmentata* similar to that shown on Trajan's Column, with narrow, bipartite, overlapping chest plates with rivets at the end of the shoulderguards. Contemporary with Trajan's Column was the Great Trajanic Frieze, which may also have originated in Trajan's Forum but which was ransacked mercilessly to adorn later monuments, most notably the Arch of Constantine next to the Colosseum. The sculptors of the Great Trajanic Frieze were clearly less constrained than those of Trajan's Column, since they depicted citizen troops wearing mail and scale as well as segmental armour. Trajan's Column had a profound influence on other sculpture too, and not just the derivative Marcus Column erected to commemorate Marcus Aurelius' Marcomannic Wars (AD 166–80), as numerous other metropolitan reliefs seem to have used it as a source in preference to accurate observation of real armour.

From this it should be clear that the reliefs on the helical frieze of Trajan's Column are not a near-photographic record of the Dacian campaigns or the equipment used on them, but have to be interpreted with great care in order not to misunderstand what is being shown. For that reason, archaeological

Groller's sketches of (above) *lorica segmentata* on Trajan's Column and (below) how he thought the pieces he found at Carnuntum should be reconstructed. (Author's Collection)

evidence has been vital in the accurate reconstruction of *lorica segmentata* in particular. Thus it was only at the end of the 19th and beginning of the 20th centuries, when serious archaeological excavations on Roman military sites began to recover examples of this type of armour – notably on the legionary fortress at Carnuntum (near Bad Deutsch-Altenburg, Austria) and the fort of Newstead (Scotland) – that progress could be made. Carnuntum was excavated by an Austro-Hungarian artillery officer, Maximillian von Groller-Mildensee (usually known by modern scholars just as Groller) and that work uncovered a rampart-back building (possibly an *armamentarium*) full of Roman military equipment of various types (Groller 1901). One room included numerous fragments of *lorica segmentata*. Indeed, there was so much ferrous corrosion product that voids in it preserved the outline of shelving upon which the armour and other material had evidently been stored. Groller devoted part of his report to these finds and included an analysis of how he thought the segmental body armour worked. Influenced by the reliefs on the helical frieze of Trajan's Column, he decided that it had been fixed to a leather jerkin of some kind in order to make it work in the way illustrated on Trajan's Column (Groller 1901: 98). These attempts to understand articulated plate cuirasses using the reliefs as their starting point were inevitably doomed to dismal failure, however. Even so, scholars persisted in using the reliefs on the helical frieze of Trajan's Column as a guide to how the armour worked, usually with unfortunate results (Webster 1960).

It was not until the discovery of elements of a number of segmental cuirasses at Corbridge (England) in 1964 that a complete, working reconstruction of two principal variants of *lorica segmentata* became feasible. It was undoubtedly helped by the fact that the armourer involved – Henry Russell Robinson – was a specialist on articulated oriental armour. The Corbridge discovery also made it possible for Robinson to reinterpret the Newstead fragments, using his newly acquired understanding of the structure of this type of armour. The beginning of the 21st century saw a number of finds that elucidated the workings of the articulated plate armguard (*manica*) in much the same way.

Unfortunately, no such key finds have as yet been made for Roman muscled cuirasses. Although there is a considerable amount of representational evidence in the form of reliefs, statues, and even wall paintings, these are almost invariably over-simplified in much the same way as the reliefs on Trajan's Column. Here, the problems encountered reconstructing *lorica segmentata* from sculptural evidence alone should caution against taking what little can be derived too literally or dogmatically.

Regal Period

We know next to nothing about early Roman armour. This bald and rather negative statement can to some extent be mitigated by pointing out that quite a lot is known about contemporary armour from elsewhere on the Italian peninsula (Burns 2005). A panoply of arms and armour from a burial at Lanuvium, about 30km south-east of Rome and dating to the first half of the 5th century BC, represents the equipment of an early Roman foe and includes a copper-alloy muscled cuirass and helmet. It is not unreasonable to assume that the Romans were extremely familiar with, and probably used, such defences. This does not alter the fact that there is no surviving Roman plate armour from the early period, however, and there is no way of knowing if it differed substantially from that of the Romans' neighbours.

A warrior's panoply, including a muscled cuirass, from a burial at Lanuvium, some 30km south-east of Rome, and dating to the first half of the 5th century BC. (Ursus/ Wikimedia/Public Domain)

Republican Period

The earliest surviving examples of plate body armour that can be attributed to the Roman Army of the Republican period were the circular *pectoralia* found in the 2nd century BC camps around the hill town of Numantia (Spain). A *pectorale* (often now referred to as a *kardiophylax*, following the Greek historian Polybios, who described it, but who has sometimes been misinterpreted as saying it was square) was a copper-alloy disc with concentric corrugations that was worn, as its name implied, over the heart of an infantryman. As such it was definitely at the economical end of the armour compromise. The discs were surrounded by a number of small holes, used to attach strap fittings (some of which still survive) to hold them in place, but the rest of the apertures may have been employed to rivet some sort of padded textile or leather backing in place, similar to that found on Italian triple-disc breastplates (Burns 2005: 57).

Polybios, himself an eyewitness to the mid-2nd-century BC Roman Army in action, described the use of this type of armour:

> The common soldiers wear in addition a breastplate of copper alloy a span [228mm] in diameter, which they place in front of the chest and call the heart-protector (*kardiophylax*), this completing their accoutrements; but those who are rated above ten thousand drachmas

RIGHT
A copper-alloy *pectorale* or *kardiophylax* from Room P in Camp II at Castillejo, the Roman base near Numantia (Spain), retaining two of its attachment plates to which straps were fixed. (Photo © Römisch-Germanisches Zentralmuseum, Mainz/S. Steidl)

FAR RIGHT
Engraving from Iustus Lipsius' (Just Lips') volume *De Militia Romana* showing the first published use of the term *loricae segmentatae*. (Author's Collection)

LORICÆ SEGMENTATÆ

wear instead of this a cuirass (*thorax*) of mail. The *principes* and *triarii* are armed in the same manner except that instead of the *pila* (*hyssos*) the *triarii* carry long spears (*doru*). (Polybios, *Histories* 6.23.14)

Here Polybios introduced an additional factor into the armour equation: cost. A small disc of copper alloy took far less time to produce – and therefore cost less – than a coat of mail. A disc found in the so-called Camp of Marcellus at Numantia measured 170mm in diameter, while another example was 175mm.

The technological leap from simple plate armour like this to the overlapping articulated plates of *lorica segmentata* is difficult to explain on the currently available evidence. Articulated armguards were certainly known in the Hellenistic period (see p.34), but the suspicion that there may be a Late Republican origin for full cuirasses is perhaps fuelled by pieces of the Kalkriese variant of *lorica segmentata* from Dangstetten (Germany), datable to 9 BC at the latest (see p.11).

Terminology

The Romans termed all forms of body armour '*lorica*', qualifying the noun (when it suited them) with an adjective, '*hamata*' for mail and '*squamata*' for scale, but what they called segmental armour remains a mystery. The term '*lorica segmentata*' was coined during the Renaissance when scholars began to study monuments – particularly Trajan's Column – in some detail. The earliest attested use of this neologism is in Just Lips' 1596 work *De Militia Romana*, which was a commentary on the *Histories* of

A | **THE PRINCIPAL TYPES OF *LORICA SEGMENTATA***
The three main types of *lorica segmentata* cuirass can be seen here, both in their component parts and complete. All three types share certain common elements: they are constructed as four units: two upper and two lower, with hinged shoulderguards and collar plates, as well as the overlapping girth hoops with the lowest pair of hoops left unfastened. The Kalkriese (**1**), Corbridge types A (**2**) and B/C (**3**) and Newstead (**4**) types are shown alongside a speculative reconstruction of the hybrid Alba Iulia type (**5**). Such a side-by-side comparison demonstrates how natural the evolution from the earliest to the latest form of this type of armour actually was.

Assuming six girth hoops for each set of armour, the component count for the various types differs slightly, with the Kalkriese type having 30 ferrous plates and 160 copper-alloy components, while the Corbridge type had 38 and 172 respectively, and the Newstead type 34 and 174. These numbers were only ever approximate (and standardized on seven girth hoops apiece) once modifications and repairs, such as attaching two fittings with one rivet, are taken into consideration.

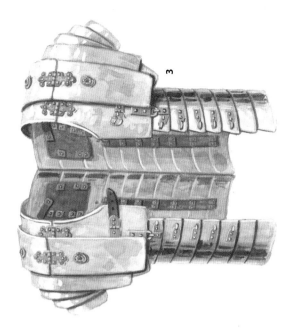

1

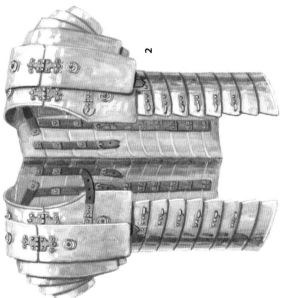

2

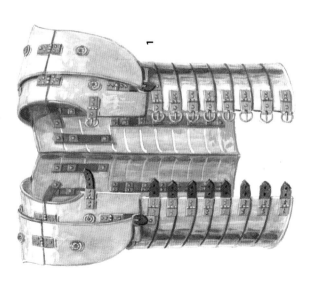

3

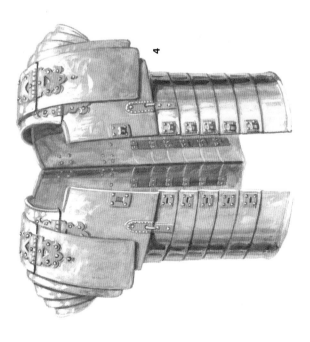

4

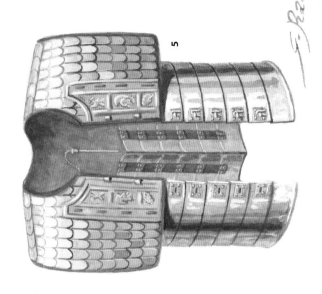

5

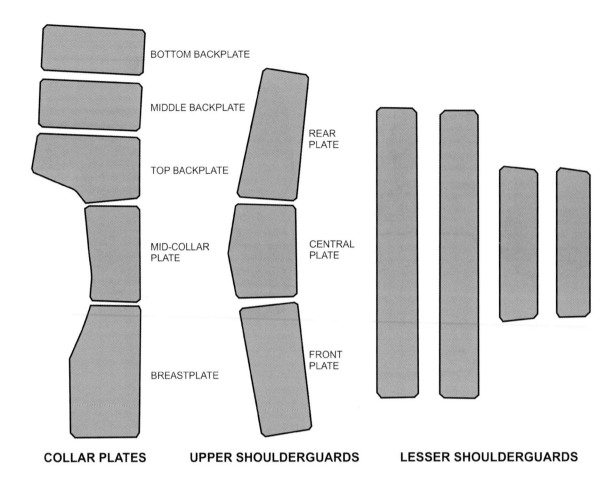

BOTTOM BACKPLATE

MIDDLE BACKPLATE

TOP BACKPLATE

MID-COLLAR PLATE

BREASTPLATE

REAR PLATE

CENTRAL PLATE

FRONT PLATE

COLLAR PLATES **UPPER SHOULDERGUARDS** **LESSER SHOULDERGUARDS**

The terminology used in describing the components of *lorica segmentata* (from Bishop 2002). (Drawing © M.C. Bishop)

Polybios and was heavily influenced by the reliefs on the helical frieze of Trajan's Column. Just Lips used the term (both in his text and to caption an illustration) without explanation, however, suggesting that he was not the first to do so:

> *Lorica segmentata*
> Finally, on another subject, what was frequently found in the time of Statius and Silius? The body was encircled with pieces of iron, arranged like bands one over the other. I confess that I have not read of this anywhere: but on the column of Trajan this type [is used] constantly and almost exclusively for Roman soldiers. (Lipsius 1630, 132 – Liber III Dialog. vi, tr. author)

The true origins of the term probably lie soon after the study of Trajan's Column began in the early 16th century with Jacopo Ripanda being lowered down from its balcony to sketch the reliefs.

The Greeks used the word θώραξ (*thorax*) to mean any sort of cuirass, but when the Romans transliterated and borrowed it (as the Latin substantive *thorax*), they seem exclusively to have meant a muscled cuirass. The coinage '*lorica musculata*' is modern and was invented (so far as it is possible to be sure) by re-enactors. It would probably have been incomprehensible to Romans, however, since the Latin words for mouse, mussel and muscle all share a common etymology.

KALKRIESE-TYPE
LORICA SEGMENTATA

In 2018, after many years of both smaller and larger components being discovered at Kalkriese (Germany), the most complete find ever of a single set of segmental body armour was made during a new campaign of excavations (Crossland 2020). This site has long been associated with the *clades Variana*, when the Roman commander Quinctilius Varus lost three legions during a rebellion led by native German troops serving as his auxiliaries (McNally 2011). As such, the date of that disaster, AD 9, has inevitably been attached to the site, although the story was undoubtedly complicated by looting by the German tribes and a subsequent visit in AD 15 by a force led by Germanicus (Tacitus, *Ann.* 1.61–62).

History

The first form of Roman segmental body armour for which evidence has been found is the Kalkriese-type *lorica segmentata* (Bishop 2002: 23–29). Earlier examples exist than those found at Kalkriese, however. Once it was realized that the Kalkriese finds belonged to this early form, it was possible to identify pieces of the same type from the base at Dangstetten, which was constructed around 15 BC and abandoned by 9 BC, two decades before the earliest possible date for the Kalkriese material. The Dangstetten fragments clearly hint that segmented body armour was in use before 9 BC, but the date of its introduction is, for the time being, unknown, although it was clearly prior to 9 BC and possibly even before 15 BC.

The Kalkriese form of *lorica segmentata* remained in use until sometime after the Claudian invasion of Britain in AD 43. Characteristic components have been identified from a few Roman military sites in southern Britain, including Chichester and Waddon Hill (both in England) (Thomas 2003: 63), both of these associated with the campaigning of *legio II Augusta* under its commander, Flavius Vespasianus. None are known from Flavian sites in the north of Britain, however, so the Kalkriese type seems to have been completely phased out by the second half of the 1st century AD. Another possible late

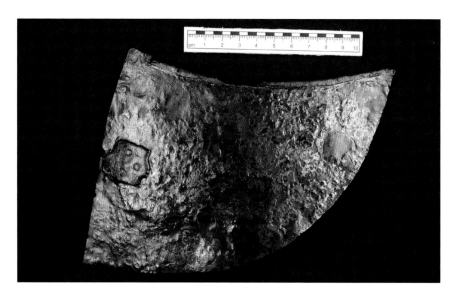

The first Kalkriese-type *lorica segmentata* upper shoulderguard component, excavated at Kalkriese itself, showing the inward-curving, almost hooked end of the plate, edged with copper-alloy piping. (Photo © Varusschlacht im Osnabrücker Land)

example of this type may be a top backplate from Rißtissen (Germany) re-used as part of a Corbridge-type cuirass. Fittings or plates from this early form of cuirass are also known from the legionary base at Vindonissa (Windisch), Kaiseraugst and Oberwinterthur (all in Switzerland), Dangstetten and Kempten (Germany), Nijmegen (Netherlands), Magdalensberg (Austria), Astorga and Iruña (both in Spain) and Novi Banovci (Serbia). Finds from Strasbourg (France) are especially interesting, given that it was the base for *legio II Augusta* before it moved to Britain in AD 43.

BELOW

Kalkriese-type *lorica segmentata* fittings from Kalkriese (**1–2**, **6–11**), Strasbourg (**3** & **5**), Chichester (**4**), Vindonissa (**12**) and Hod Hill (**13**). (Drawings © M.C. Bishop)

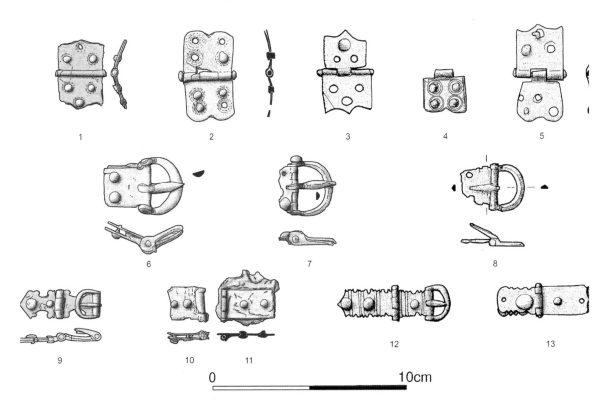

Description

There were four basic units that made up segmental body armour and this was to remain true of all the subsequent main forms. There was a shoulder section in left and right halves and a torso section, also in left and right halves. Each of these four elements was riveted to its own internal leather harness.

A series of ferrous collar plates – breastplate, mid-collar plate and top backplate – surrounded both sides of the neck and were joined together by copper-alloy hinges riveted to the plates at the points where they overlapped slightly. The inner edges of these plates, next to the wearer, were turned out. The backplate was shorter than the breastplate, so two additional plates were hung below it, joined by internal leather straps, to provide the same depth of protection at the back as at the front. The leather straps were riveted to the interior faces of the plates by means of copper-alloy rivets which passed through the plate and leather and which were then peened over (sometimes using internal

OPPOSITE

Left top backplate, mid-collar plate and breastplate from the complete *lorica segmentata* found during the 2018 excavations at Kalkriese. (Photo Hermann Pentermann, © Varusschlacht im Osnabrücker Land)

The first Kalkriese-type *lorica segmentata* breastplate, showing how the mineralized leather straps of the horizontal and vertical fasteners were riveted directly to the ferrous plate. Whether these are the original fittings or a repair is unclear. (Photo © Varusschlacht im Osnabrücker Land)

roves). Above these, and attached by means of internal leather straps with rivets, were three upper shoulderguards: front, middle and back. As with the collar plates, these overlapped slightly and were joined together by hinges. The front and back upper shoulderguards curved inwards towards the centre of the thorax. The centre plate broadened and curved downwards over the shoulder slightly. These were the only forms of shoulder protection and the upper arms were left unprotected, just as they were with mail or scale cuirasses. The left and right upper halves were joined together using single buckles on each of the breastplates and backplates. There is clear evidence from finds from Kalkriese itself that some of the copper-alloy fittings were tinned or silvered.

The abdomen was protected by a series of overlapping ferrous bands, now usually known as girth or girdle hoops. The number of these – usually between five and seven – seems to have varied not as a distinguishing mark of different variants as was once thought (Robinson 1975: 177), but rather to provide the best fit for the individual. These bands overlapped top to bottom and were joined together by means of three internal straps for each half, with straps riveted to the plates at the front, back and side. The two halves were joined together by means of a series of external buckles, both front and back, set against the lower edge of each plate.

The top and bottom sections of the cuirass were fastened together with external buckles, one for each breastplate and the lowest of the three backplates on either side.

Many of the ferrous plates that made up a Kalkriese cuirass were edged with copper-alloy piping in much the same way that contemporary Roman helmets were. Although it provided a decorative touch to the armour, this was in fact a simple way of avoiding having to finish the edges of the plates too carefully, since it was far less time-consuming just to apply such piping than to finish the edges. The piping was placed in areas which could come into contact with (and possibly damage) the wearer's underlying garments. The copper rivets which attached the internal leather straps to the ferrous plates on the upper (but not the lower) sections might also have been supplied with decorative washers, once again matching those used on contemporary helmets.

No actual organic leather has survived on any of the recovered examples, but examples of mineralized leather straps have been found. When large amounts of ferrous material are deposited in the right ground conditions, the corrosion products seep into the cells of any attached organic material over time and thus 'fossilize' them as they rot in a process known as mineralization.

B

SEGMENTAL ARMOUR IN USE AT KALKRIESE

Although *lorica segmentata* was not the only form of body armour used during the sporadic fighting with German warriors in AD 9, it had become important to the legions of Germany even before Varus led three of them beyond the Rhine. Several different variants can be seen at the same time in this scene of an attack on a Roman temporary camp during the long march through hostile territory, as well as the more familiar mail (which covers more of the lower body than the segmental cuirasses). Two basic forms can be seen here, but there is also clear evidence of repairs and even cannibalization. The first form uses simple rectangular fittings, while the second has more elaborately decorated hinged buckles and strap fittings. A third is a hybrid, however, with some of the hinged fittings replaced by straps riveted directly to the armour plate. Yet another is mostly of the first kind but with one upper unit taken from the second. Cuirasses may ultimately have acquired additions by their owners in the form of additional plates over the tops of the arms. This sort of field modification would eventually become incorporated into the later Corbridge type. The method of fastening the girth hoops would also ultimately change, and it is possible that the original hinged buckles would have been removed and the rivet holes used to lace plates together with leather thongs (many of the soldiers can be seen with spares tied to their cuirasses for just such eventualities).

Variants

An interesting range of variants of the Kalkriese form can be identified (types A and B – Bishop 2002: 23). One of the first pieces found, a left-hand breastplate, had both horizontal and vertical fastening straps riveted directly onto the ferrous plate with large, flat-headed rivets. Whether this was a crude repair to a piece that originally had copper-alloy fittings, or whether it pre-dated such embellishments is impossible to tell. The complete set of armour found in 2018 used simple hinged, rectangular buckle plates to attach buckles to their respective armour plates and rectangular hinges to join the shoulderguards and collar plates. More elaborate hinged buckle plates with serrated edges have also been found at that same site, however, and it is these, together with the characteristic sub-lobate hinges that joined collar and shoulderguard plates together, that have been found in Britain. It is tempting to see a development from simple to complex fittings, but in reality all may have been in use at the same time and these variations may just reflect the work of different armourers or even the handiwork of different legions. Equally, shoulder hinges seem to have presented a problem from the very beginning: the number of rivets was increased from three on each hinge half to four (and was to be increased again with the Corbridge type).

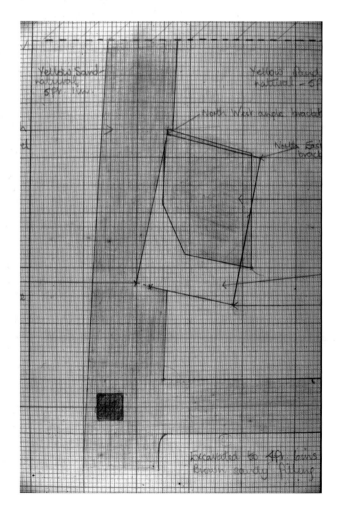

Plan of the Corbridge Hoard made during the excavation in 1964, with north towards the top. The lid (in grey) was originally thought to be floorboards overlying the chest. (Photo © M.C. Bishop)

CORBRIDGE-TYPE *LORICA SEGMENTATA*

A full understanding of how *lorica segmentata* functioned only became possible after a find during training excavations at the Roman site of Corbridge, just 2km south of Hadrian's Wall (Robinson 1975: 174–80, Figs 178 & 180). In 1964, the remains of a wooden box packed full with a wide range of items was discovered and lifted in a block for subsequent examination in a museum laboratory. The finds from the Corbridge Hoard chest included six sets of lower halves, and six of upper halves, of *lorica segmentata*, seemingly collapsed for ease of storage. It was this find that enabled Charles Daniels and Henry Russell Robinson finally to solve the mystery of how segmental body armour was put together (Daniels in Allason-Jones & Bishop 1988: 97–100).

The Corbridge type incorporated a number of major changes over the Kalkriese type, all of which seem to have been improvements based on experience. First, the method of fastening the girth hoops, using buckles and straps (with the hinged buckles and straps contributing up to 48 moving parts), was simplified into the new pairs of static tie loops. Second, the method of attaching the upper and lower assemblies changed at the rear from one external to double internal buckle-and-strap pairs. Third, the lesser shoulderguards were added to protect the tops of the shoulders, the upper shoulderguards being accordingly reduced in width and straightened out. Fourth, the collar plates, including the breastplate and backplates, were reduced in width. Fifth, the number of rivets attaching hinges to a plate on the upper shoulderguard was increased to five for each half, leading to the characteristic lobate shape that is nowadays so familiar for *lorica segmentata*. Finally, all copper-alloy piping on the edges of plates was done away with, the edges being rolled instead, while the corners of plates were clipped.

History

The earliest finds of Corbridge-type *lorica segmentata* have been made at Magdalensberg (Austria) and date to the early Claudian period, when the Roman Army seems to have abandoned the site (Thomas 2003: 91). Its use was certainly common by the time of the invasion of Britain, some of the earliest British finds coming from the Roman military occupation of the native dyke system at Colchester Sheepen (England) (e.g. Thomas 2003: 82). It then became the principal form of this armour throughout the rest of the 1st century AD and into the 2nd. Excluding the Corbridge Hoard material, major finds of armour of this variant include a set of girth hoops from St Albans (England), most of an upper assembly from Plantation Place in London (along with a cut-down and extremely well preserved breastplate from the Bank of England site), much of the cuirass of a legionary thought to have been killed during the attack on Gamla (Israel), as well as a collection of components from Rißtissen which, had Robinson seen them when they were first found, might have helped him solve the puzzle of segmental armour much earlier. Significant assemblages of *segmentata* plates and fittings are also known from Richborough (England), Caernarfon (Wales) and Svishtov (Novae, Bulgaria).

Finds of the Corbridge form are the most common and widespread, and the available dating evidence indicates that it continued in use until at least the latter part of the 3rd century AD in some places (Aurrecoechea 2003/04: 52).

Right-hand *lorica segmentata* breastplate from the Bank of England site, next to the Walbrook in London, showing damage received to the plate, which has subsequently been scrapped and cut down. (Photo © M.C. Bishop)

The Corbridge Hoard

In 1964, a training excavation at the Roman site of Corbridge in Northumberland (England), just 2km south of Hadrian's Wall, made a spectacular discovery while examining the remains of a 2nd-century AD fort: what became known as the Corbridge Hoard. The remains of an iron-bound wooden chest containing a wide variety of items were located and carefully lifted in a block by the excavation supervisors (a process which had to be completed under car headlights!) for later examination in laboratory conditions. The bulk of the material in the box had been iron, although all that remained were corrosion products. The process of mineralization (see p.14) had preserved a range of organic materials, including wood, leather, textile, bone, feathers, and even scraps of papyrus. The items in the chest had been carefully packed and it is thought that it was intended for departing troops to take it away with them and that, for whatever reason, it ended up being left behind and buried, presumably to deny the raw materials to any enemy.

Among the contents, and carefully wrapped in cloth, were the components of the *lorica segmentata* which would enable the director of the excavations, Charles Daniels, and the armourer Henry Russell Robinson, to reconstruct for the first time exactly how this type of armour had functioned – even using cardboard templates cut out of breakfast cereal packets in order to understand the finer points. The armour, which had been collapsed and compressed to take up as little room as possible when packed, included six upper (three left and three right) and six lower sub-units (again, three left and three right). These very roughly corresponded to enough sub-units to make two Corbridge type A/B and one type C cuirasses, although if they had been put together they would have looked rather mismatched. All of the sub-units showed signs of damage and repair, sometimes repeatedly carried out.

The limited available evidence indicated that the wooden chest was buried in the first half of the 2nd century and probably towards the end of the reign of the Emperor Hadrian (r. AD 117–38).

Description

As with the Kalkriese types, the Corbridge form of segmental body armour consisted of two upper and two lower halves, each riveted to its own internal leather harness.

Once again, a ferrous breastplate, mid-collar plate and top backplate encompassed both sides of the neck, but were now joined together by elaborate lobate copper-alloy hinges, which were riveted to the plates at the point of overlap with five rivets on each half. Those edges adjacent to the wearer were turned out once again but, in the absence of copper-alloy piping, also rolled inwards to form a rounded edge. The backplate was still shorter than the breastplate and had two additional plates beneath it, once more joined by internal leather straps. Above the collar plates, and attached to them with internal leather straps, there were three upper shoulderguards at the front, middle and back, which also overlapped slightly and were joined together by lobate hinges. The shape of these shoulderguards was very different from that of their predecessors, however. The middle plate was narrower and the front and back plates were straight-sided, not curving as on the Kalkriese form. In addition, four new lesser shoulderguards were added on either side, attached to the upper shoulderguards by internal straps, providing protection for the upper arms. The left and right upper halves continued to be joined together using single hinged buckles on the breastplate and each of the backplates.

The abdomen was again protected by a series of overlapping girth hoops, between five and seven in number. These bands also overlapped top to bottom and were joined together by means of three internal straps for each

OPPOSITE

Corbridge-type *lorica segmentata* fittings, including lobate hinges from Sheepen (**1**), Rheingönheim (**2**), Chester (**3**), Hofheim (**4**) and Oberstimm (**5**); decorated washers from Silchester (**6**), Rheingönheim (**7**), Longthorpe (**8**), Chichester (**9**) and Chester (**10**); hinged buckles and hinged strap fittings from Sheepen (**11**), Carnuntum (**12**), Chichester (**13**), Oberstimm (**14** & **16**), The Lunt (**15**), Rheingönheim (**17**, **20** & **22**), Broxtowe (**18**), Aislingen (**19**) and Vindonissa (**21**); and tie loops from Hod Hill (**23** & **25**), Carnuntum (**24**), Rißtissen (**26**), The Lunt (**27**), Rheingönheim (**28**) and Corbridge (**29**). (Drawings © M.C. Bishop)

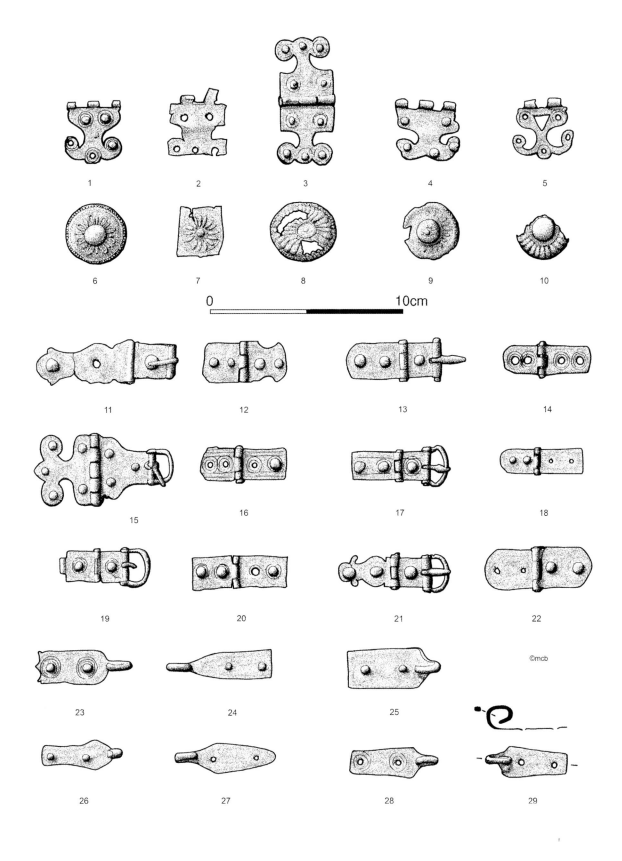

1 2 3 4 5

6 7 8 9 10

0   10cm

11 12 13 14

15 16 17 18

19 20 21 22

23 24 25

©mcb

26 27 28 29

half, with straps riveted to the plates at the front, back and each side. The two halves were now fastened together by means of a series of tie loops, both front and back, which were riveted to the underlying ferrous plates. As with the Kalkriese form, these tie loops were set flush with the lower edge of each plate but, unlike the earlier type, the lowest two hoops were left without fasteners. The other fasteners were used to secure the lower sub-units with knotted leather laces and vastly reduced the number of moving parts employed over the earlier type.

The top and bottom sections of the cuirass were still fastened together with strap-and-buckle combinations in the Corbridge type A variant, one external on each breastplate, but now with two internal ferrous examples on each of the lowest of the three backplates on either side. The B/C variant introduced a new means of attaching the top half of the cuirass to the lower: a metal hook-and-eye system (copper alloy on the B, ferrous on the C) with two at the front and four at the back.

None of the ferrous plates of a Corbridge cuirass were edged with copper-alloy piping, suggesting that time was now taken to finish the edges of the plates, but in reality these were often just rolled, turned out, or both. The corners of ferrous plates tended to be clipped to help blunt the point. The copper rivets attaching the internal leather straps to the ferrous plates invariably included decorative washers of a similar type to those found on contemporary helmets.

The mineralization of the organic components allowed a complete reconstruction of the leathering regime that acted as a flexible matrix for the armour. It was clear how copper-alloy rivets passed through ferrous plates from the front, through the leather, and were then peened over, sometimes (but not always) through square or rectangular roves on the inside. Repairs were evident and in one place two separate internal leather straps on the three backplates of an upper section had been replaced by one large patch.

Variants

It was Robinson who devised the A/B/C naming system for the Corbridge form of the armour. The type A variant was characterized by external, hinged, copper-alloy buckles joining the upper and lower sections at the front, accompanied by internal ferrous buckles at the back. The upper

C   CLEANING CORBRIDGE-TYPE ARMOUR

Part of a Roman legionary's life was always spent in maintaining his arms and armour, whether in his quarters in a legionary fortress, or out on campaign. Sitting on the veranda of the barracks at Isca Silurum affords these men of *legio II Augusta* the chance to spend some time looking after their kit after a recent patrol. A legionary had to be fastidious in how he cleaned both the metal and leather components, since moisture – whether from rain or sweat – was the enemy of an effective set of armour. He not only had to remove corrosion from the surface of the ferrous plates as well as from the brass fittings, but also clean carefully around the vulnerable points where those fittings made contact with the ferrous plate. That was not the end of the job, however, as it was then necessary to check every rivet holding the metal plates to the internal leather

strapping and oil the leather to keep it supple and resilient; any that was damaged had to be replaced. Rather than work on a complete cuirass, each soldier breaks his armour down into its four constituent units which he rests upon his knee, one piece at a time.

This is not the only routine maintenance being undertaken, since helmets had to be cleaned just as carefully, swords sharpened with a hone, and boots checked for any broken straps or missing hobnails – and it is clear from the archaeological record that Roman soldiers shed hobnails in alarming amounts. A painstaking inspection of the *contubernium* leather tent now, in barracks, could save the need for later unwelcome repairs in the field. Any items in need of more serious repair would be set aside for later attention from the legionary workshop.

shoulderguards were of a uniform width from front to back. The B/C variants differed in having broader middle upper shoulderguards, which swelled to a point. They also used a different means of attaching the upper and lower sections: instead of vulnerable buckle-and-strap junctions they employed simpler, external, hook-and-eye fittings. Robinson distinguished type B from C by means of these fittings, the former made of copper alloy and the latter ferrous, but in reality the truly significant difference lay between the strap-fastened A and hook-and-eye B/C, particularly in light of subsequent developments with the Newstead type.

One unusual adaptation was found on the remains of a cuirass from Gamla (Stiebel 2014: 67), for which the internal leathering joining the three backplates on each side was replaced (on one side only) by a system of sliding rivets of a kind that would not be seen again until its use in medieval plate armour. This is the only known example of this variant, so it may just have been a local variation (like the large leather patch, see p.20) rather than a separate type; it was certainly a replacement for the original leather straps since their rivets were still *in situ*. An example of an upper shoulderguard found at Chichester, and associated with the early campaigns of *legio II Augusta* soon after the invasion of Britain in AD 43, demonstrated the use of double rivets to secure the internal leathers, while an upper backplate from the same site had oval roves for the leathering rivets.

A reconstructed set of Corbridge-type *lorica segmentata* broken down into its four component units with the girth hoops stacked inside the shoulder sections in much the same way as in the Corbridge Hoard. (Photo © M.C. Bishop)

View of the internal leathering of a reconstructed Corbridge-type *lorica segmentata* shoulder section with the rivets peened over square roves. (Photo © M.C. Bishop)

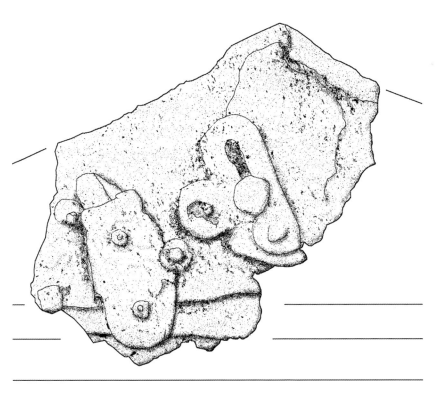

0 _____ 10cm

Interior face of Corbridge-type *lorica segmentata* backplates from Gamla showing internal leathers replaced by sliding rivets. (Drawing © M.C. Bishop)

NEWSTEAD-TYPE
LORICA SEGMENTATA

This, the third major form of articulated cuirass, is named from the site in lowland Scotland where a significant collection of parts was found at the beginning of the 20th century (Curle 1911: 156–58, Fig. 11 & Pl. XXII). Although early attempts were made to reconstruct this form of armour, it was not until the Corbridge discovery was made that it was finally understood (Robinson 1975: 180–82, Fig. 181). Even then, some details were missing, and it only became clear from subsequent finds that this form also used lobate hinges, albeit much larger ones than earlier examples (some examples were already known from the Carnuntum find but were not recognized as having come from a different form).

Just as the Corbridge type incorporated a number of improvements over its predecessor, so the makers of the Newstead form sought to address issues which the Corbridge type had in turn introduced. Chief among these (although not one Robinson recognized, because the Newstead find had no such pieces) was the increase in size of the lobate hinges on the upper shoulderguards and collar plates, presumably to counter the twisting moment between the plates by making the hinge itself broader. The second major improvement was the replacement of the triple backplates with one large plate, corresponding to the breastplate (which was also increased in size compared with its predecessor). Third, a new method of fastening both breastplates and the new backplates was introduced. Finally, the troublesome nature of the girth hoop fastenings required attention again, so the pairs of

The Newstead well

Like most headquarters buildings (*principia*) in Roman forts, the stone fort of Trimontium at Newstead included a well in its courtyard. It is often suggested that this had a ritual purpose, so it is unsurprising that the fill of such wells is sometimes viewed as having a special significance by archaeologists. Excavated in September 1905, the well at Newstead (designated Pit I by its excavator, James Curle) was 7.8m deep, and 6.1m in diameter at the top and almost 2m at the bottom. It contained a variety of interesting items in its fill (Curle 1911: 47–48, 116–17), leaving little room for doubt that it had been deliberately backfilled at the time of abandonment.

Near the top was a large deposit of rubble (including a fragment of an inscription), presumably designed to seal off the material that lay beneath. There was more stone throughout the fill of the well. At a depth of 1.5m, some fragments of jewellery. At 3.66m, a stone altar to Jupiter and a coin of Hadrian were found, with animal bones and leather, including shoes, at 4.27m. At 5.49m, there was a stone moulding, along with sherds of amphorae and Samian ware. At 6.4m there was an iron bar, while at 6.7m, there were two human skulls, brass scale armour, and more sherds of amphorae and Samian ware.

At the bottom (and so the first material to be thrown in), besides the eponymous *lorica segmentata*, there was the upper stone of a quern, two iron knives, a linchpin, the staves and bottom of an oak bucket, the iron rim of a large bucket, a large block of sandstone bearing a relief of a boar (the emblem of *legio XX Valeria Victrix*), five iron arrowheads, some mail armour, an iron shield boss, fragments of brass, a coin of Vespasian or Titus, a holdfast of iron, a fragment of wall plaster, and amphora sherds.

The presence of arms and armour in the fill of the *principia* well has been used to argue that the rooms surrounding the courtyard served as a magazine (*armamentarium*), but since the other material accompanying the weaponry must have been derived from other areas of the fort, this is unconvincing.

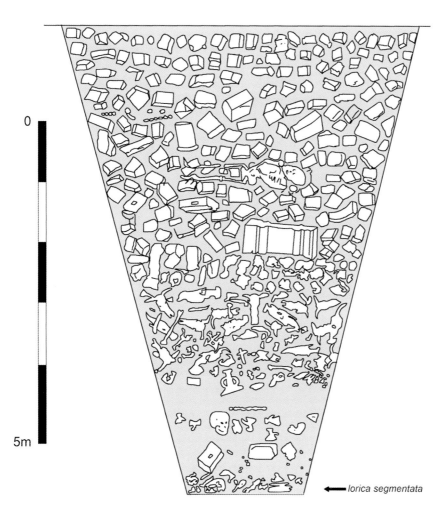

← *lorica segmentata*

tie loops were abandoned and yet another system was introduced, this time incorporating cast copper-alloy loops passing through the opposing plates and thereby minimizing movement between the halves. To judge from the numbers of cast loops that appear in the archaeological record, this last innovation brought its own problems.

History

Although the find from Newstead itself can be dated to soon after the middle of the 2nd century AD (the site was abandoned by around AD 180), there is good reason to suspect that this type of armour was being introduced towards the end of the 1st century AD. The Carlisle Millennium backplate came from a Hadrianic deposit within the Roman fort at Carlisle (England), but a large lobate hinge from the timber legionary fortress level of Ulpia Traiana Sarmizegetusa (Romania) is probably Trajanic (Băeştean & Barbu 2015: Pl. IV.1). It became the dominant form of *lorica segmentata* by the second half of the 2nd century AD, a fact attested by finds of this form from Eining (Germany), Newstead itself, León (Spain), Carlisle (in two strikingly

The components of the original Newstead-type *lorica segmentata* found in the *principia* well (Pit I) at Newstead itself. (Drawings © M.C. Bishop)

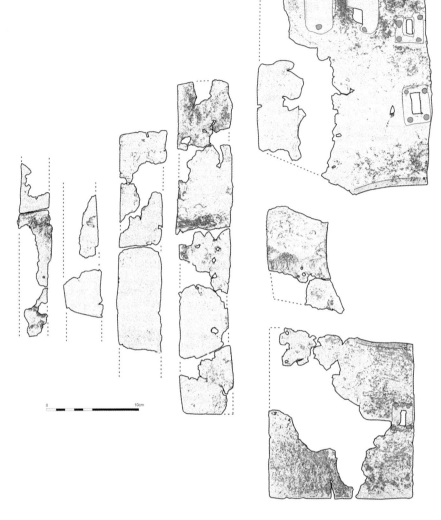

different contexts), Caerleon (Wales), and at Stillfried (Austria), as well as from the former cavalry fort (later regarrisoned with infantry) at Aalen (Germany). It continued in use in some areas into the 4th century AD, as the discoveries from Carlisle (Caruana 1993) and León (Aurrecoechea 2003/04: 52–53) have revealed.

D **NEWSTEAD ARMOUR AT THE TYPE SITE**

In the latter part of the 2nd century AD, the fort of Trimontium at Newstead was abandoned by the Romans, sometime after the retreat from the Antonine Wall further to the north. The process of dismantling a fort was particularly thorough and quite distinct from any damage an enemy attack might cause, with buildings systematically dismantled and any resources that might be of use to an opponent rendered inaccessible. In the case of Newstead, this involved dumping material into pits and wells, including the well in the corner of the courtyard of the headquarters building, which was where the *lorica*

segmentata fragments were found. The armour was obviously in need of repair and was probably being kept for recycling or cannibalization purposes. In this reconstruction, the process of filling the well has just begun, while in the background the demolition of the building is already under way. Since not all of the material found in the well would have belonged in the *principia*, it must have been brought from nearby and that will have affected the order in which items were discarded. Legionaries are using the wicker baskets they normally employ for removing soil from excavations, such as when ditch digging, to carry the material that requires disposal.

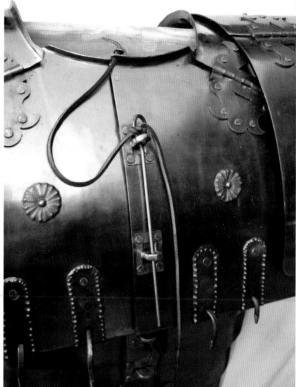

ABOVE LEFT
A Newstead-type backplate dating to the Hadrianic period from the Carlisle Millennium excavations. (Photo © Pascal Lemaire)

ABOVE RIGHT
Detail of a reconstructed Newstead-type cuirass showing the backplates fastened using two turnkeys and a vertical cotter pin, attached to the turned neck by a thong. (Photo © Arik Greenberg)

Description

The Newstead type of *lorica segmentata* followed its predecessors by retaining the two upper and two lower halves. As with the other forms, each of these elements was riveted to an internal leather harness. Substantial differences were introduced in the detail of the cuirass, however.

There were ferrous breastplates and mid-collar plates as before, but now the earlier three backplates were replaced by a single, large backplate that now matched the breastplate. The three collar plates were still joined together by copper-alloy lobate hinges, but they were now much larger than before. As before, there were three upper shoulderguards at the front, middle and back, which overlapped and were joined together by the new, larger form of lobate hinge. These shoulderguards were situated above the collar plates and were once again attached to them with internal leather straps. Although no upper shoulderguards have as yet been found, the new large hinges supply a minimum width for them and the simplest reconstruction sees the larger Corbridge plates (with a central point) continued. Four lesser shoulderguards were added on either side, as before, and were attached to the upper shoulderguards by internal straps. A major change was the manner in which the left and right upper halves were joined together. This was now accomplished by means of one turnkey on the front plate and two on the rear.

The abdomen was again protected by a series of girth hoops, between five and seven in number. These bands also overlapped top to bottom and were joined together by means of three internal straps for each half, with straps riveted to the plates at the front, back and sides. The means by which

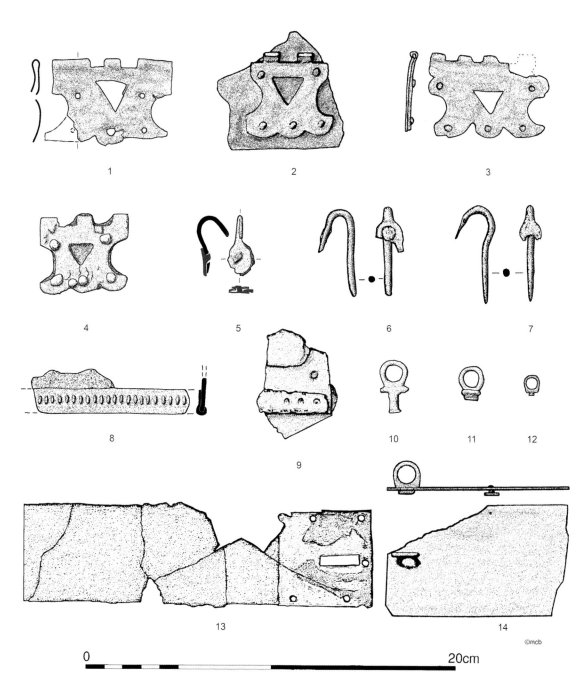

the two halves were fastened together changed again, now using cast rings attached through the ferrous plate with shanks which were peened over to the rear, with one of the plates having an aperture to allow the lower loop to pass through (presumably still fastened with knotted leather laces, although split pins on a thong would also have worked). To judge from the number of examples found in the archaeological record, the tie rings seem to have been very vulnerable and prone to becoming detached. The ends of the plates with the apertures were either faced with copper-alloy sheathing riveted to the front or had a smaller surround to the opening of this metal. Overall, this new structure made for a more rigid hoop than had previously been

Newstead *lorica segmentata* fittings, including lobate hinges from Carlisle (**1**), Carnuntum (**2**), León (**3**) and Sarmizegetusa (**4**); vertical fasteners from Carlisle (**5**) and Iža (**6** & **7**); girth hoops from León (**8**), Iža (**9** & **13**) and Carnuntum (**14**); and girth hoop tie rings from Carlisle (**10**), Newstead (**11**) and Iža (**12**). (Drawings © M.C. Bishop)

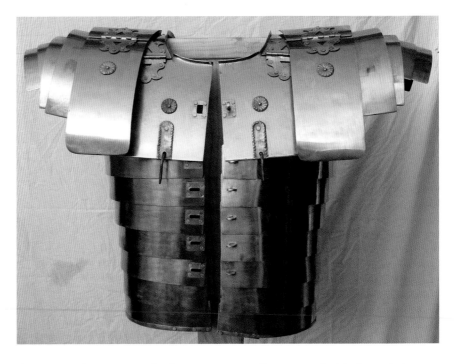

Reconstructed Newstead-type cuirass with the front open showing the larger lobate hinges, vertical fasteners, the turnkey-and-slot horizontal fastener on the breastplate, and the loop-and-slot girth plate fasteners. (Photo © Arik Greenberg)

The Stillfried *lorica segmentata* girth hoops on display in the site museum. (Wolfgang Sauber/Wikimedia/ CC BY-SA 4.0)

the case and mounting the fastening centrally was probably intended as an improvement over the Kalkriese and Corbridge fastenings on the lower edge.

The top and bottom sections of the cuirass were once again fastened together with a similar metal hook-and-eye system to that found on the Corbridge B/C variant, with one on either side of the breastplates and two on the backplates. One unusual detail of the Stillfried cuirass fragments was an additional pair of ferrous hooks mounted externally at the side and pointing upwards, possibly to support the wearer's belt, although this is purely speculation.

Unlike the Corbridge form of the cuirass, some use was made of copper-alloy piping, perhaps to reduce the time taken to finish the plate edges. The clipped corners of the ferrous plates of the Corbridge type were now replaced by simply rounding them. The copper rivets attaching the internal leather straps to the ferrous plates could include decorative washers, but this was not always the case.

Variants

Robinson believed that all Newstead cuirasses had fewer girth hoops than their Corbridge predecessors, but the find from Stillfried makes this assumption unlikely. Fragmentary girth hoops from Zugmantel on the German limes do indeed display a deeper lower plate, however, so this may be an indication of a separate variant from the Stillfried finds, unless it is part of a hybrid cuirass (see p.31).

OTHER FORMS OF PLATE ARMOUR

Two additional forms of articulated plate armour have been suggested from iconographic evidence and these may be termed 'hybrid' forms. Articulated plates were also used as limb defences, most commonly armguards. Single- or double-plate greaves were known throughout the Roman period, while head and breast protection for horses also used metal plates.

Hybrid forms

The principal behind articulated plate armour seems to have been applied to other forms of armour to form composite hybrids of the various technologies. A sculpted relief of a soldier from Alba Iulia (Romania), with the curved, rectangular shield characteristic of a legionary, is of particular interest here (Bishop 2002: 62–66). He is clearly a soldier rather than a gladiator (the tip of his sword scabbard and its chape are visible: gladiators did not use scabbards) and is depicted wearing a form of armour comprising metal bands around his abdomen, along with scale on his shoulders and the kind of breastplates regularly found fastening later mail and scale shirts. The piece probably dates to the later 2nd or early 3rd centuries AD, since the sword is worn on the his left hip. He also wears a segmented armguard on his sword arm (see p.34). This hybrid cuirass raises a very interesting question: would it necessarily be recognized in the archaeological record from its components if they were not found still attached (Bishop 2002: 62–65)?

Assuming this to be an at-least-partially accurate representation of a genuine form of cuirass, rather than a misunderstanding on the part of the sculptor, it begs the question of why this amalgamation of two different forms of armour might have been thought necessary. It may have been a genuine attempt to do away with the problems of the shoulder assembly, but it is also possible that it is in fact a pragmatic cannibalization of available parts to produce a functioning piece of body armour when resources were limited: a one-off that was not found anywhere else.

The Alba Iulia example is not the only potential hybrid cuirass depicted on sculpture. A relief from Arlon (Belgium) shows cavalrymen in action. They appear to have been depicted wearing mail on the torso but – in a reversal of the Alba Iulia sculpture – this has been interpreted as having plate upper shoulderguards like those of *lorica segmentata* (Bishop 2002: 72–73). The problem here is that the sculpture is sufficiently ambiguous that while one observer might see plate shoulderguards, another might identify the standard folded shoulder doubling found on other cavalry mail cuirasses. The question of whether plate armour at this point might have been more or less effective than simple mail doubling is clearly open to debate, but having only one ambiguous representative source is, at the very least, problematic. Comparison with a second relief from

Relief from the legionary fortress of Apulum at Alba Iulia depicting a soldier with a curved, rectangular shield; an articulated armguard on his sword arm; a hybrid form of cuirass with segmental bands around his torso; and scale armour over his shoulders, which is fastened with breastplates. (Photo © J.C.N. Coulston)

What appears to be a Kalkriese-type top backplate re-used in a Corbridge-type cuirass from Rißtissen. (Drawing © M.C. Bishop)

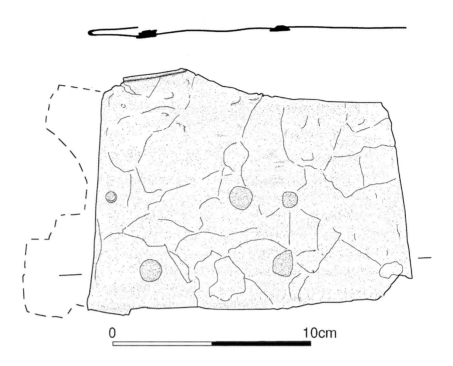

Arlon, together with one from Liège (Belgium) and a number of cavalry tombstone reliefs, all of which show standard shoulder doubling, does little to assist the argument for segmental shoulderguards attached to mail cuirasses (Bishop 2002: 72).

In both cases, an actual example of a hybrid cuirass would help clarify the uncertainties outlined here and it is not impossible that such a find may one day occur. There is, however, a form of hybrid cuirass that is well attested and incorporates a small amount of plate armour: later mail and scale cuirasses. During the 2nd century AD, at a time of great innovation in Roman military equipment, both mail and scale armour are known with central pairs of breastplates. For a long time dismissed as 'parade armour', it is now realized that it was practical, saw everyday use, and just happened to be decorated; and the Alba Iulia relief is, coincidentally, the only depiction of such plates. The plates had the same basic L-shaped form, produced by removing a curving section from a rectangle to accommodate the neck. They were reinforced by careful use of corrugation, in the form of a raised border and internal panel divisions, as well as by the embossed decoration itself. The standard mythological motifs appeared (see p.51) but they sometimes also incorporated unit identifiers, specifically when they had belonged to legionaries. This type of breastplate was, obviously, used in pairs, nicely demonstrated by a right-hand plate from Mušov

E **THE ALBA IULIA TYPE IN 3RD-CENTURY DACIA**

Legionaries face up to attacking Goths outside the *porta praetoria* of the fortress of Apulum in order to give a returning patrol time to get to safety. Commanded by the senior centurion, the *primus pilus*, who wears a muscled cuirass in recognition of his newly achieved equestrian status, they wear a variety of different forms of armour, including mail, scale, both Corbridge and Newstead types of *lorica segmentata*, and a hybrid Alba Iulia cuirass, with a scale top, and girth hoops and shoulderguards harvested from previously damaged segmental armour. The returning troops mostly wear mail and scale but the centurion leading them has a set of pristine Newstead armour.

(Czech Republic), inscribed LEG[io] X, above a representation of a bull, the totemic animal of *legio X Gemina*, together with a left-hand plate from Orgovány (Hungary) bearing the inscription GEM[ina], likewise above a depiction of a bull. Another (incomplete) right-hand plate from Carnuntum bore images of an eagle and a figure of Mars with the full title LEG[io] XIIII GEM[ina] for the legion based in that fortress. The missing lower register probably included the legionary totem, the capricorn. These pairs of plates were fastened by overlapping them and then passing a turnkey attached to the lower plate through a slot in the upper plate. The rotated turnkeys could then be held fast by a long cotter pin or a pair of split pins on a thong. Examples of these turnkeys are quite common individually but some have also been found still attached to a lower plate, as on an example from the Carlisle Millennium excavations (Bishop in Howard-Davis 2009: 691, Fig. 338). There does not seem to have been a preference as to which plate, left or right, should be the lower or upper.

There was also a form of single, symmetrical plate attached to mail and scale, often flared outwards towards the base, and similarly decorated with embossed mythological scenes. These have much smaller neck cut-outs at the top and, as with the much shallower neck openings on backplates of Newstead-type *lorica segmentata*, they may have been attached to the rear of a cuirass. Such a plate comes from Ritopek (Serbia) and is covered in decorative motifs, including two centurial standards, a *vexillum*, Mars, and busts thought to depict various martial personifications (such as a *genius legionis* and *virtus*). A piece belonging to a mail shirt from Bertoldsheim (Germany) is of this shape but is actually formed from one narrow and one broad plate and served as a closure.

Armguards

Laminated arm defences were known in the Hellenistic period, with an example excavated from Ai-Khanoum (Afghanistan) (Bishop 2002: 18), although the true origins of this form of limb defence, as with body armour, may lie even earlier with steppe peoples.

In the Roman period, the intimate relationship between legionary and gladiatorial equipment is readily apparent in the form and use of the articulated armguard (*manica*). Armguards provided protection for the sword arm, which was normally held close to the side of the body, but when striking was extended and vulnerable. Although representational evidence, especially reliefs, can be ambiguous and difficult to date accurately, wall paintings make it clear that two types of arm defence were used. The first was a padded fabric form, worn on both arms and legs, and generally shown as light in colour. The second was a metallic defence, normally of overlapping metal plates. Murals found at Pompeii (Italy) make it clear from the use of colour and the subtle treatment of the reflection of light by the artist that this latter form was in use by gladiators before the destruction of that town in AD 79. While mail and scale *manicae* are attested in the arena, however, they do not seem to have been adopted by the Roman Army.

The convenient *terminus ante quem* provided by the eruption of Vesuvius is unusual and most gladiatorial depictions are difficult to date precisely. Legionary tombstones, on the other hand, are often easier to place within a time range. Thus it is that two legionary tombstones from Mainz, belonging to Sex. Valerius Severus and G. Annius Salutus, depict a range

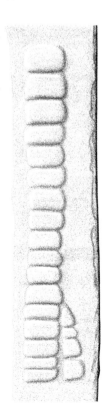

Depiction of an armguard on the tombstone of Sex. Valerius Genialis. (Drawing © M.C. Bishop)

of equipment in relief around the inscriptions. Legionary movements are fairly well understood, thus it is possible to determine that these pieces date to between AD 43 and AD 70, when *legio XXII Primigenia* was based at Mainz. Although it might be objected that the tombstones actually show gladiatorial equipment, the presence of a *pilum* makes this unlikely. This confirms that *manicae* saw use in at least one unit in the Roman Army during the second half of the 1st century AD. This is interesting, not least because it has in the past been suggested that armguards were first introduced during Trajan's Dacian Wars at the beginning of the 2nd century AD specifically to counter the fearsome, scythe-like *falx* used by Dacian warriors. Armguards are depicted on the sword arms of legionaries on the sculpted panels or metopes of the Tropaeum Traiani at Adamclisi in Romania (AD 108–09). The reliefs on the helical frieze of Trajan's Column, on the other hand, do not show armguards in use. The latest depiction of an articulated armguard is on the Arch of Severus at Leptis Magna (Libya). This probably dates to *c*.AD 203 and shows armguards in use with *lorica segmentata* (J. Coulston, pers. comm.).

Fragments of articulated armguards were found at the beginning of the 20th century at both the legionary fortress at Carnuntum (ferrous) and at Newstead (copper alloy), although they were not correctly identified at the time of discovery. Some extremely significant discoveries have been made in more recent times, particularly in the deposit in the fort at Carlisle (see p.38).

Simplified diagram illustrating the internal leathering of an armguard, with the leathers attached to the interior of each lame with a rivet. The larger circles are apertures for the attachment of a removable, padded lining. (Drawing © M.C. Bishop)

0   10cm

Carlisle Millennium ferrous Armguard A showing both exterior (left) and interior (right) views with cross-sections. The lowest four or five plates (down to the wrist) were missing when deposited. (Drawings © M.C. Bishop)

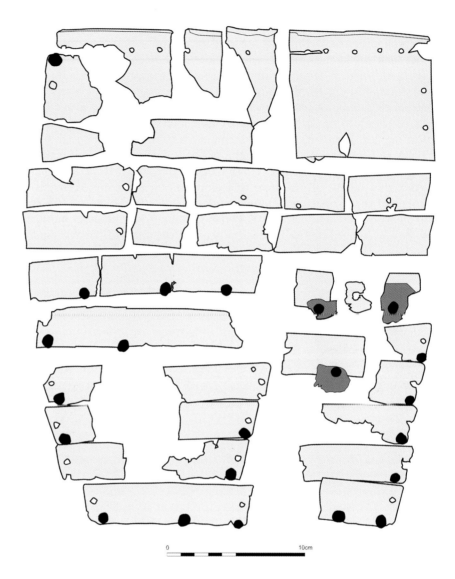

The copper-alloy plates from the Newstead armguard, found in the fort headquarters building. (Drawing © M.C. Bishop)

0   10cm

Located within what appeared to have been a workshop, elements of three ferrous arm defences were excavated among an anaerobic deposit that contained a wide range of organic material, as well as the three arm defences, still articulated when they were discarded. These finds confirmed that the plates on such a defence overlapped upwards, from wrist to shoulder, unlike articulated body armour, which overlapped downwards.

F ARMGUARDS IN COMBAT IN DACIA

Roman legionaries in hand-to-hand combat with Dacians outside the walls of the Dacian hilltop capital, Sarmizegetusa Regia, during the Second Dacian War (AD 105–06). Wearing mail and scale body armour, as shown on the metopes of the Tropaeum Traiani at Adamclisi, and *lorica segmentata* as depicted on Trajan's Column, they are all equipped with laminated arm defences on their sword arms and greaves on both shins. It is clear how, when a legionary reaches forward to strike an opponent and exposes his sword arm, the laminated armguard lies along the top of his arm to protect it against downward blows. Similarly, the greaves worn on the leg are a vital defence against a low swing from a two-handed *falx*, the lethal weapon favoured by the Dacians. Damage is visible on both body and limb armour, some of it quite severe, whereas a tribune to the rear of the legionaries, wearing a well-polished muscled cuirass of copper alloy, is slightly safer from the blows of their opponents. Some of the legionaries could have worn of the latest Newstead-type cuirasses.

The Carlisle *manicae* (Bishop in Howard-Davis 2009: 694–700) had apparently been articulated on leather straps fastened to the plates with rivets and roves but, despite the excellent state of preservation, none of the leather straps survived. Arguably the most important revelation from the Carlisle finds was the extent to which all of the armguards had been repaired, in some cases multiple times (see p.54).

Other finds have been made in the legionary base of León (ferrous, end of the 3rd century AD: Aurrecoechea et al. 2008) and in what was apparently an auxiliary fort at Till-Steincheshof in Germany (copper alloy, late 1st or early 2nd century AD: Brüggler et al. 2012). A near-intact ferrous example from the legionary base at Sarmizegetusa Regia (Grădiştea de Munte, Romania) remains unpublished. All of these examples confirm that the metal plates overlapped upwards from the wrist to the shoulder. Further fragments of plates, readily identifiable as deriving from *manicae*, are known from Roman military sites at Corbridge, Richborough and Eining. Overall, there was little difference between the earliest and latest surviving examples, although the Carlisle armour had clipped corners, while those of the León piece had rounded ones, much like the plates on contemporary segmental cuirasses.

The archaeological evidence from these various finds has provided detailed information on the structure of this type of arm defence. The same method of construction was used regardless of the metal employed. The top plate was always the largest (45mm wide on one Carlisle example) and incorporated some means of attaching the defence – a hook or a ring – either to the body armour or to some sort of harness passed around the upper body of the wearer. This was essential to stop the defence rotating on the arm when in use (Aurrecoechea et al. 2008: 261). The upper edge was also turned outwards and at the same time rolled inwards, just as on some plates from Corbridge-type cuirasses. The strips of metal (often referred to as 'lames') below the top plate ranged in width between 28mm and 36mm (28–34mm on one Carlisle *manica*, 31–36mm on another) although they were not always consistent in width, some varying by as much as 3mm over their length. The actual lengths of the lames varied in a more uniform manner: the shortest plates were found near the wrist, getting progressively longer the higher up the arm they were situated. The terminal plate at the wrist end

Reconstruction of the Newstead copper-alloy armguard produced by Peter Connolly for the Trimontium Trust. (Photo © M.C. Bishop)

was the shortest – just 100mm long, tapering to 70mm, on the León example (Aurrecoechea et al. 2008: 259, Fig. 5) – and flattest, since it just had to cover the back of the hand. These plates were wrapped around the arm by bending to form a horseshoe-shaped section, but they did not completely enclose the arm, thus avoiding the need for a couter plate at the elbow. Rivets (both copper-alloy and ferrous on the Carlisle examples) along the upper edge of each plate served to attach them to the internal leather straps upon which they were articulated. A minimum of three straps was employed (one at the centre and one towards either end), but this was often increased to four on the upper arm, where the plates were longer. The Carlisle plates were found in associations that showed that they were still articulated when deposited although, despite the deposits preserving tanned leather extremely well, the armguard internal leathers themselves were no longer present except as small patches of mineral-preserved matter around the rivets. Similarly, no substantial traces of lining nor means of fastening the defence around the arm were found (although they could have been stripped away, leaving just the plates joined to the internal straps). This indicates that, as with *lorica segmentata* (see p.49), the internal leathers were probably not made of tanned leather.

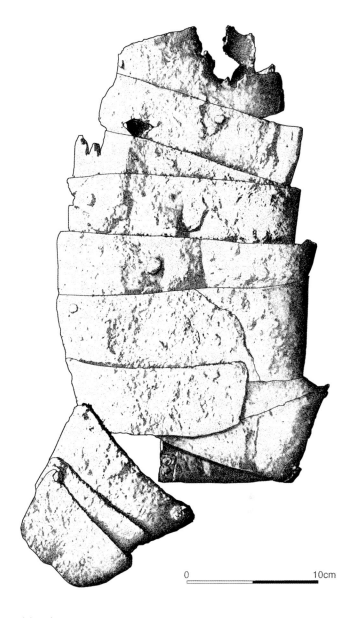

Forearm section of a ferrous armguard, still articulated, excavated from the legionary fortress at León, and dated towards the end of the 3rd century AD. The smaller plates over the wrist clearly illustrate how laminated armguard plates overlapped upwards towards the top of the arm. (Drawing © M.C. Bishop)

The upward-overlapping plates of the defence were designed to deflect blows towards the crook of the arm, where the plates would concertina when the arm flexed, thereby enhancing local protection. The armguard thus sat along the top of the forearm and front of the upper arm when the wearer was holding a sword.

Besides the lames themselves, there would be a large plate at the top of the arm from which the other plates were ultimately suspended. At least one of the Carlisle examples incorporated metal tie loops and rings which may have been related to the means of attachment of the armguard. All surviving examples have additional small holes on the sides and along the top of the large upper plate, indicating that the defence had a lining attached; and some examples have been found with fragments of leather attached.

Muscled cuirasses

For the Romans, the definitive 'uniform' of the officer classes – the senators and equestrians who were appointed to command military units, provincial armies, and even rule the empire itself – was an idealized imitation of Hellenistic equipment. Moreover, there has to be a suspicion that it was intended to imitate the equipment of one man in particular: Alexander the Great of Macedon (r. 336–323 BC). For this, the plate cuirass was a central component, but our understanding of this form of armour is hampered by an absence of any complete examples available for study. There are many examples of cuirassed statues, both in stone and cast bronze, and arguably no finer example than the statue of Augustus from the Villa of Livia at Prima Porta (Italy). These provide many tantalizing details, but an excavated cuirass of the Republic or Principate has yet to be recovered.

A remarkable example of a Hellenistic iron cuirass was excavated from a tomb at Vergina (Greece) and is often attributed to Philip II of Macedon (r. 359–336 BC), the father of Alexander the Great. Rather than a muscled cuirass, however, this was an imitation in iron of a Classical Greek linen cuirass or *linothorax*. A representation of Alexander wearing a metal cuirass (to judge from the attempted depiction of reflections on the lower part of his torso) is to be found on a mosaic from Pompeii depicting the battle of Issus (333 BC) and generally agreed to be a faithful copy of a painting by Aristides of Thebes or Philoxenus of Eretria. Alexander's armour features a *gorgoneion*, a depiction of the head of the gorgon Medusa, in the centre of the breast. This served an apotropaic purpose to protect the wearer and it is a common detail to be found on emperor statues. His cuirass also features shoulder pieces like those on Philip's iron corselet. It is noteworthy that Alexander is not shown wearing a muscled cuirass, since there is no attempt to imitate idealized pectoral or *rectus abdominis* muscles.

An actual example of a Hellenistic ferrous muscled cuirass, probably dating to the early 3rd century BC, was excavated from a tomb at Prodromi

BELOW LEFT
Detail of the mosaic from the House of the Faun in Pompeii depicting Alexander the Great at the battle of Issus with a *gorgoneion* in the centre of his breastplate. (Berthold Werner/Wikimedia/Public Domain)

BELOW RIGHT
Copper-alloy Etruscan or Greek muscled cuirass of the 4th century BC from Ruvon (Italy). (© The Trustees of the British Museum)

(Greece) and is much more obviously the model for the cuirasses depicted on emperor statues. Equipped with shoulder tabs, which were tied to the chest by means of rings on the gilded nipples, it lacked the *gorgoneion* so beloved of emperor statues. It also seems that the front and rear halves were attached by means of ties through rings fixed below the armpits on either side.

All cuirassed statues depicted emperors wearing this piece of armour during the Roman period, rather than a segmental, mail or scale cuirass (Stemmer 1978). The two forms were a low-abdomen, shaped form for men on foot, while those on horseback had higher, horizontal lower edges to enable them to sit more comfortably (Bergemann 1990). As such, emperors were attempting to depict themselves as part of the officer class, rather than as ordinary soldiers. The high quality of such depictions, whether in stone or bronze, means that the main components of the muscled cuirass are known. It consisted primarily of the front and back plates, joined on either side beneath the armpit apertures. The front plate was usually decorated with a *gorgoneion* between the emphasized pectorals: an apotropaic representation in relief of the gorgon Medusa's head, famed for turning any who beheld it to stone. The shoulders of the front plate were also ornamented with faux doubling, similar to that found on real mail and scale cuirasses, tied down to rings on the emphasized nipples. Since no muscled cuirasses survive, however, it is not possible to tell if these were hinged to the front or rear plate, although the latter might make more sense. The means of securing the front and rear plates is inevitably simplified on statues, although a bow on the visible side of the Prima Porta Augustus suggests they may have been tied together. The cuirass was finished off

ABOVE LEFT
Statue of Augustus from the Villa of Livia at Prima Porta near Rome, wearing an elaborately decorated muscled cuirass highlighting the return of one of Crassus' lost eagles. (Till Niermann/Wikimedia/Public Domain)

ABOVE RIGHT
Relief generally thought to come from the Arch of Claudius in Rome and now in the Louvre in Paris. Although heavily restored (note the anachronistic moustache), it may depict members of the Praetorian Guard, at least two of whom appear to be officers wearing muscled cuirasses. (Christophe Jacquand/Wikimedia/CC BY-SA 4.0)

Funerary tondo in the museum at Graz, originally from Seggauberg (Austria), depicting an officer wearing a muscled cuirass and holding a sword in his left hand and (possibly) a *vitis* in his right, suggesting he might be a centurion. (IKAl/Wikimedia/CC BY-SA 2.5)

with a sash tied around the body at the junction between the thorax and abdomen, and invariably worn with *pteryges* (strips terminating in tassels) at the shoulders and around the midriff. Although it was once thought that the *pteryges* were attached to the armour, it is now generally accepted that they belonged to a garment worn beneath the armour and over the tunic which is possibly to be equated with the *thoracomachus* of the literary and sub-literary sources (see p.57).

It is important to remember that the number of muscled cuirasses in circulation at any one time was unlikely to have been large. With only around nine officers per legion likely to have worn one (*legatus, praefectus castrorum*, the six *tribuni* and perhaps the *primus pilus*, who had attained equestrian status) and presumably just one (the *praefectus* or *tribunus*) in every auxiliary unit, the chances of even one surviving are slim. An Antonine funerary tondo from Seggauberg (Austria) depicts an officer (possibly a centurion, to judge from the *vitis* (the vine wood staff of office) he is holding) wearing a muscled cuirass, which might have increased the number if this practice was widespread at that time. It is also not just a case of numbers: the differential for survival between mail and segmental body armour (see p.51) is a known problem, but the factors affecting large items like a muscled cuirass, with only two major components, are completely unknown.

Depiction of a muscled cuirass with *pteryges*, spear and *vexillum* on a relief from the Temple of Hadrian in Rome. (José Luiz Bernardes Ribeiro/ Wikimedia/CC BY-SA 4.0)

Greaves

Defences for the lower leg, in the form of greaves (*ocreae*), were employed sporadically by the Romans throughout their history. Their use meant that, when a legionary was in the customary 'at the ready' pose, with the left leg advanced, shield held in front just below eye height to protect the torso, helmet to protect the head, the last vulnerable exposed part of his body – the left shin below the lower edge of the shield – was protected by a greave. The use of only one greave was to be found in both infantry and gladiators for the same reason: protecting the right shin was less important than the left. Polybios recorded that the *hastati* 'have two *pila*, a copper-alloy helmet, and a greave' (Polybios, *Histories* 6.23.8).

No greaves survive from the Republican era, but the components of a device excavated from the fortress at Cáceres el Viejo (Spain), generally held to be the Castra Caecilia of Q. Caecilius Metellus Pius, dating to around 78 BC, were interpreted as a greave press for producing these items from sheet metal (Mutz 1987).

Under the early Principate, we find that depictions of centurions on gravestones regularly included greaves that covered the knee. The greaves of the centurion T. Calidius Severus from Carnuntum were depicted with human faces on the knees, echoing a classical tradition found on some Greek examples and also perpetuated on Roman cavalry greaves with knee protection. Those of M. Favonius Facilis, a centurion of *legio XX* who died at Colchester (England) within a decade of the invasion of Britain, were plain, but the greaves of Q. Sertorius Festus from Verona (Italy) incorporated a decorative, vegetal design, presumably embossed into the metal. Other centurions' gravestones, e.g. an unattributed fragment from Burnum (Croatia) or M. Pompeius Aspro from Labico, near Rome, choose to only display the attributes of the man, so instead of a full-figure relief of the deceased, distinctive elements such as a transverse helmet crest, the *vitis* and greaves are shown, clearly implying that, at this time, greaves were the mark of a centurion.

The situation had changed by the beginning of the 2nd century AD, and possibly even earlier than that. The Adamclisi metopes unequivocally

Plain, undecorated copper-alloy greave (unprovenanced). Height 357mm. (Photo P. Gross © Arachne)

43

0   10cm

Plain, undecorated iron greave from Carlisle dating to the Hadrianic period. Height 314mm. (Drawing © M.C. Bishop)

OPPOSITE
Decorated cavalry greaves from Straubing. Height 499mm (left and right). (Wolfgang Sauber/ Wikimedia/CC BY-SA 3.0)

illustrate legionary troops wearing pairs of greaves. One interpretation of this might be that encounters with the scythe-like *falx* used by Dacian warriors had inspired the Romans to adopt lower leg defences, along with the laminated armguard, for enhanced protection from this weapon. That, however, overlooks the fact that an earlier (pre-Flavian) tombstone of C. Annius Salutus (*CIL* XIII, 6953) from Mainz has a decorative frieze surrounding the inscription which depicts, among a variety of pieces of legionary equipment, greaves and an armguard.

Actual finds of greaves from the first half of the 2nd century AD have also been made. The same excavations at Carlisle that produced a deposit containing armguards (see p.35) also contained a greave (Bishop in Howard-Davis 2009: 700), which was Hadrianic in date. Possibly contemporary is an assemblage of items reputed to have come from a cave in Hebron (Palestine), which included an iron Weisenau-type infantry helmet, a mail shirt and two iron greaves, all tentatively dated to the time of the Bar Kochba Jewish uprising of AD 132–36 under Hadrian (Weinberg 1979). Unlike hoplite greaves, which were shaped to fit the shin and calf without any form of fastening, Roman greaves only ever covered the front part of the shin and required a fastening, usually in the form of three ring-and-tie attachments near the top, middle and bottom, to hold them in place. Rather than being half-round in section, these greaves were often formed with a central ridge, presumably to provide extra strength and enhanced resilience to blows to the front of the shin, but it may also have made them easier to produce.

As with any form of plate armour, some form of lining was essential for both comfort and blunt-force shock absorption (see p.57), and at least two possible leather greave linings were found during excavations in the midden outside the fortress at Vindonissa.

This form of infantry greave continued into the 3rd century AD, examples coming from a hoard of equipment found at Künzing (Germany) that was probably buried at the time of the Alemannic invasions of AD 233 or 259/60 (Garbsch 1978: 47). This period also saw the introduction of cavalry greaves designed for use in the cavalry training and display exercises known as the *hippika gymnasia*. These greaves were both elaborately decorated, with embossed mythological elements, and structurally different to earlier forms, since the knee and shin covers were now separate and joined by a hinge. Probably dating to around the same time as the Künzing find, another hoard of equipment found near Straubing (Germany), the fort (named Sorviodurum) of a part-mounted cohort (as yet unidentified) on the Danube, included six cavalry greaves with knee protectors (Garbsch 1978: 48–49) – Roman infantry greaves did not need to cover the knee because of the length of the shield, but the knees of cavalrymen on horseback were more vulnerable. Ownership inscriptions showed that two of the Straubing greaves had belonged to men in the *turma* of Moronus. They were decorated with a variety of embossed motifs (see p.51). Other decorated greaves are known from frontier sites, but none in the same concentration that was found at Straubing.

By the time of the Dominate, greaves had largely passed out of fashion once more, and the Late Roman writer Vegetius only describes them in the context of their past use by his idealized *antiqua legio* (Vegetius *De Re Militari* 1.20, 2.15).

Horse armour

The Romans did not use plate horse armour in combat but they did find a place for it in the *hippika gymnasia* as protective headgear (chamfrons or shaffrons) for the horses. These are mentioned by Arrian in his description of those cavalry exercises:

> The horses are carefully protected with chamfrons (*prometopidia*). On the other hand, they do not need side armour, because the javelins used in those exercises do not have iron tips, so they could injure the horses' eyes, but hardly their flanks, especially since these are largely protected by a saddle cloth. (Arrian, *Techne Taktike* 34.8, tr. MCB)

Chamfrons (Garbsch 1978: 13–14, 85–88, Taf. 44–48) were by no means a Roman invention, and they were depicted on Hellenistic friezes (often subsequently mimicked in Roman reliefs). In the 1st and early 2nd centuries AD, leather chamfrons were used, since they only had to provide protection against soft-tipped practice weapons. Formed from two layers of leather (one goatskin, the other cow, both skin outwards), it has been argued that, since these were of double-thickness leather, they would have been made of toughened leather, formed over a last and treated with heat (Dobson 2018: 7). Although these leather chamfrons were decorated with patterns of studs

Copper-alloy eyeguard that would originally have been attached to a leather chamfron to protect a horse's eye during the *hippika gymnasia*. (Photo © National Museum of Antiquities, Leiden)

A tripartite 3rd-century AD copper-alloy chamfron with large central plate and side plates from the Straubing Hoard. The central plate depicts a bust of Mars beneath an eagle, while the side plates are decorated with lunate designs below the integral eyeguards. An inscription showed that this belonged to Tertius in the *turma* commanded by Ianuarius. (Wolfgang Sauber/ Wikimedia/CC BY-SA 3.0)

A tripartite copper-alloy chamfron with a smaller, hexagonal, central plate and side plates from the Straubing Hoard, dating to the 3rd century AD. Both the central plate and the eyeguards depict the head of Ganymede, the eyeguards being pierced to enable the horse to see through them. An inscription recorded that this was the property of the *duplicarius* Primitivus. (Wolfgang Sauber/Wikimedia/CC BY-SA 3.0)

and small appliqués, they featured perforated copper-alloy eyeguards for the horse. The development of a metal form during the 2nd century AD allowed far greater range in embossed decoration. Without the survival of some of the leather chamfrons, however, these copper-alloy eyeguards would be the only evidence for such defences.

Most of the upper part of a one-piece copper-alloy chamfron decorated with a lion's head is known from the legionary fortress at Neuss (Germany) (Garbsch 1978: Taf. 44), but many more-complete and later examples are known from frontier forts around the empire. These originally consisted of a small plate that fitted between the eyes of the horse and which was hinged to perforated eyeguards similar to those used with leather chamfrons. The central plates became larger and were matched by larger side pieces incorporating perforated eyeguards. These provided much more scope for the sort of decorative detail involving deities and heroes beloved on 3rd century AD Roman cavalry. As with the chamfrons made of leather, they were not intended for use in battle, but rather served to protect the horse's face during the vigorous dummy missile volleys of the *hippika gymnasia*.

The Straubing Hoard produced a group of five, three-part, metal chamfrons. Each one consisted of a gently tapering frontal that rested along the nose of the horse, with a hinged plate on either side that incorporated pierced hemispheres to cover the eyes of the horse while still permitting it some degree of vision. Each chamfron has some means of attachment to the head of the animal, some in the form of integral loops, others as free-moving rings attached to the periphery. Presumably these were attached to the regular bridle used for the horse, although given the unusual nature of *hippika gymnasia* equipment – specifically designed not for combat but for this unusual and colourful combination of training and display – it cannot be ruled out that they had their own specialized bridle used just for this purpose with dedicated attachment points for a chamfron.

The question of whether copper-alloy saddle horns could be regarded as a form of plate armour (protecting the vulnerable parts of both the saddle and rider), or whether they were merely a part of the structure of the saddle, remains moot.

MANUFACTURE AND DECORATION

Workshops

During the Principate the bulk of production of arms and armour seems to have rested with the Army itself. A papyrus from Egypt records work undertaken by legionaries, auxiliaries, civilians and even slaves in a legionary workshop (*fabrica*). Listing the products over two days, one item (*lamnae levisatae* or 'light plates') could well be construed as components for *lorica segmentata*, but this is of course speculative. A fragment of text by the jurist (and Praetorian Prefect) Tarrutienus Paternus preserved in Justinian's great *Digest* of Roman law recorded the range of specialists carried on staff by the legions, including coppersmiths and blacksmiths (*Digest* 50.6.7). Under the Dominate, however, there were specific *fabricae*, spread across both cities and fortresses in the eastern and western halves of the empire and tasked with producing various types of military equipment (*Notitia Dignitatum, Or.* 11; *Occ.* 9).

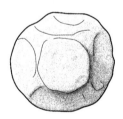

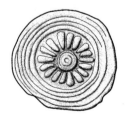

Copper-alloy stamp from Oulton used for producing embossed rosettes employed on both Corbridge-type *lorica segmentata* and Weisenau/Imperial-Gallic helmets. (Drawing © M.C. Bishop)

0   2 cm

Manufacture

There is no doubt that, to some extent, Roman plate armour had to be constructed for the individual. When Robinson made his first reconstruction of a Corbridge cuirass, basing the dimensions on those of the excavated material, he found that 'it dug-in even on my daughter's slender neck' (Daniels in Allason-Jones & Bishop 1988: 99). There could be no 'one size fits all' approach to Roman plate armour in general and *lorica segmentata* in particular.

One of the more unusual aspects of the plates used to form *lorica segmentata* is that they were technologically extremely sophisticated. Metallographic examination of surviving uncorroded plates (of which there are very few) shows them to have a harder exterior and softer interior that resembles modern mild steel. Given the available technology, however, and the fact that it might be anticipated that the plates would have been formed by working billets of iron, they are surprisingly free of the slag inclusions that might be expected. Instead, the plates that have been examined have a degree of purity suggestive of having been produced from a molten state – something generally believed not to have been possible until the invention of the Bessemer converter in the 19th century, although a similar process had in fact existed in China since around the 11th century AD. Moreover, the uniform thickness of the sheet metal (Sim & Kaminski 2012: 49–50), together with marks on the surface, points towards some sort of rolling process being used in the formation of the steel sheet (Sim & Kaminski 2012: 137). The thickness of the uncorroded London (Bank of England) breastplate is just 1mm but, as has been observed (Sim & Kaminski 2012: 138), Roman steel plate was every bit as effective as High Medieval plate twice the thickness; and this quality was available to every soldier, not just an elite few.

By contrast, the production and assembly of sets of fittings for *lorica segmentata* can seem quite crude at times, so much so that one suspects that semi-skilled labour was being used for the process: unsurprising, if legionary workshops were using legionaries, auxiliaries and civilians. The copper-alloy components were cut from thin brass sheet which, like the steel sheet of the armour, shows signs of having been rolled in order to

Two upper shoulderguard plates of *lorica segmentata* from the Corbridge Hoard that have been overlapped more than normal then riveted together, although the redundant lobate hinges have not been removed. The purple-grey colouration of the decorated rosette washers has been confirmed by pXRF as being derived from silver. (Photo © M.C. Bishop)

achieve its thinness. Riveted and hinged fittings were usually produced by doubling over the sheet before it was riveted in place, although fittings are sometimes found where only the end with the hinge is doubled over and the rest of the body is made from single-thickness brass sheet. Decorative rosette washers for rivets were stamped from brass sheet before being cut out, and stamped-but-uncut examples have been found at military sites including Rheingönheim (Germany). A stamp for producing these is also known from Oulton (England).

The brass fittings were normally fitted to the ferrous plates by means of rivets with a very high copper content, which was reflected in their colour: orange in contrast to the golden yellow of the brass. The high proportion of copper made the rivets softer and thus easier to peen over and secure in place.

It was noted earlier that, while the Carlisle deposit contained considerable amounts of tanned leather, no internal leathering survived on any of the armguards, despite their still being articulated. It is also true that no *lorica segmentata* components have been found with organic remains of leather still attached, only mineral-preserved straps. It is not unreasonable to conclude, therefore, that a form of untanned leather (such as rawhide) was used for the internal straps of both cuirasses and armguards. This must have been oiled in some way to keep it supple – if allowed to dry out the leather could become extremely hard; a property the Romans exploited when using it for shield edging in the 3rd century AD (Bishop 2020: 22).

It has on occasion been argued that both muscled cuirasses and *lorica segmentata* may have been formed from thick moulded or hardened leather, but there is no plausible evidence that this was the case. Sculpture cannot in and of itself assist with such an identification, while both finds of metal body armour in Greece and Italy, alongside colour depictions, suggest metal was the favoured material for muscled cuirasses. The absence of actual finds of leather muscled cuirasses in a Roman context is matched by a similar lack of metal examples, but given the likely limited numbers of such cuirasses in use at any one time, this is hardly surprising. By contrast, the fact that components (and even complete sets) of ferrous-plate segmental cuirasses survive in considerable numbers heavily mitigates against the use of leather for this type of armour, not least because organic armour could never have been as effective as steel at the same thickness and weight (so would have to have been heavier and bulkier to come anywhere near matching its defensive qualities), quite apart from the additional demands it would have placed upon Rome's livestock resources.

Decoration

So far as is known, there was nothing by way of decoration on the ferrous plates of *lorica segmentata*, but the appliqué fittings were another matter altogether. Made from *orichalcum* brass (the same alloy used in some coins), these looked almost indistinguishable from gold, providing they did not become tarnished. Whether it was the embossed rosettes that acted as washers for leathering rivets or the lobate hinges used to join neighbouring plates, there was a standard grammar of ornament associated with this type of armour and at least in part shared with helmet decoration under the Principate. Leathering rivet washers, for instance, could be embossed with rosette designs or concentric circles, while some examples incorporated red enamel on the rivet heads. Some of the Kalkriese fittings were tinned or silvered and pXRF analysis has shown that even the Corbridge Hoard armour included silver (or silvered) decorated washers on some upper shoulderguards (Dr F. McIntosh, pers. comm.). Rivet holes on fittings were often adorned with concentric incised rings, possibly a product of the tool used to punch the hole through the sheet metal. The plain rectangular hinges of the shoulder units on early Kalkriese forms of *lorica segmentata* quickly evolved into sub-lobate hinges and, ultimately, into lobate hinges on the Corbridge type. There was no need for such an elaborate form for these fittings, which had to be cut out from brass sheet, since all that was needed was a hinged plate that could be attached to two ferrous plates with five rivets on each half: the shape was purely decorative. Robinson (1975: 177) believed that such fittings began elaborate and eventually became cruder with time, but the elaborate openwork lobate hinges of the Newstead type disprove this hypothesis. Moreover, while the use of copper-alloy piping on the Kalkriese and Newstead types was undoubtedly primarily functional, in that it could conceal poorly finished edges that might snag on the wearer's clothes, there can be no denying that it had visual appeal too, and this was enhanced in some cases with additional decorative details such as the embossed beading of the León examples (Aurrecoechea & Muñoz Villarejo 2001/02: 20). As noted earlier, some copper-alloy fittings on the Kalkriese form could be tinned or silvered (see p.14).

It is not known how the exterior of segmental body armour was presented and whether it was highly polished or just kept clean. There is a limited amount of evidence to suggest that shiny armour was thought to intimidate an opponent, Vegetius noting: 'For the brilliance of equipment terrifies enemies. Who can believe that a soldier is warlike, if, through negligence, his arms are disfigured by filth and rust?' (Vegetius, *DRM* 2.14).

It was thought to be a mark of how decadent city-based, 2nd-century AD eastern troops had become when Lucius Verus' general, Pontius Laelianus, 'a man of character and a disciplinarian of the old school, in some cases ripped up their cuirasses (*loricae*) with his fingertips' (Fronto, *Letters to Lucius Verus*

19). Regardless of whether this refers to mail, scale or plate armour, it underlines the importance of well-maintained armour to the Romans (see below).

At the same time, little evidence survives in the archaeological record for the original condition of the interior of *lorica segmentata* and whether any forge blackening (with, for example, beeswax or olive oil) was engaged in, principally for the purposes of preventing corrosion.

Other forms of plate armour (in copper alloy, at least) made great use of embossing. Decorated greaves are regularly depicted in Roman representational art and finds of what are thought to be such greaves from cavalry sports armour are elaborately embossed and chased to show common mythological figures and deities. Examples from Straubing included Mars, Hercules and Minerva, along with eagles and dolphins (common military decorative motifs at this time).

The chamfrons from Straubing (see p. 47) also – unsurprisingly – exhibit a very similar grammar of ornament to the greaves, including embossed representations of Mars, Minerva and the Dioscuri (Castor and Pollux), along with eagles and snakes. The hemispherical eyeguards incorporated into the chamfrons were mostly pierced with a pattern of triangles, although one piece had eyeguards in the form of the pierced head of the Gorgon, with the eyes of the figure similarly pierced, meaning the horse was also looking through the Gorgon's eyes!

It is unclear whether this type of embossed decoration was usually produced by chasing from the rear against a former – a labour-intensive operation – or by some sort of stamping process, which was much closer to a form of mass production. Stamping was used for smaller items like belt plates, *lorica segmentata* decorative washers (see p.49), and even for larger items such as decorated sword scabbards (Bishop 2016: 16). The discovery of what have been identified as components of a Republican-era greave press during excavations at Cáceres el Viejo, if they have been correctly interpreted, would seem to support the possibility that embossed greaves could have been produced by stamping copper-alloy sheet (see p.44). If that was indeed the case, then it would not be surprising if the same was true of chamfron components.

The early 3rd-century AD tombstone of Marcus Aurelius Alexys from Sparta, possibly showing the girth hoops of a *lorica segmentata*. (George E. Koronaios/Wikimedia/ CC BY-SA 4.0)

Maintenance

In the archaeological record, pieces of segmental plate armour are far more common than scale or mail. Comparison with the representational record, however, suggests that this is not because it was the most common form of armour in use. Both sculpted, figural tombstones and state propaganda monuments depict scale and mail in use. The problem seems to have been that *segmentata* was much more prone to damage than either mail or scale. Careful examination of finds like those from the Corbridge Hoard usually reveals evidence of damage and repairs (both competent and botched).

In contrast, no complete examples of a muscled cuirass from the Late Republic or the Principate have survived, despite the fact that they seem to have been the preferred form of body armour for equestrian and senatorial Army officers. In fact, there are more fragments of cast bronze statues depicting the cuirasses of members of the imperial family.

These observations reveal fundamental differences between these two main forms of plate armour in use by the Roman Army. If a metal muscled

Two collar plates of *lorica segmentata* from the Corbridge Hoard, twisted out of alignment and with one original hinge half (bottom) and a larger replacement (top), which has been riveted into place with four larger dome-headed rivets, one of which has been secured centrally through a triangular cut-out instead of in either of the two available holes. (Photo © M.C. Bishop)

cuirass – with few major components – was damaged, the entire object had to be repaired; if a piece fell off of a segmental cuirass, however, the sheer number of components became advantageous, since damage to one item was unlikely to be as crucial to the whole defence as those pieces of muscled cuirass. Roman re-enactors will frequently carry with them spare lengths of leather lace with the specific purpose of being able to manage running repairs to their armour if something should break.

Quite apart from the complexity and relative fragility of its structure, every version of *lorica segmentata* had a fundamental flaw: the combination of ferrous and copper-alloy components made it vulnerable to bi-metallic corrosion, particularly if it was not carefully dried and cleaned after use. Indeed, some of the points of contact – underneath brass fittings riveted to ferrous plate, for example – could not be cleaned without de-riveting and removal, which was impractical under normal circumstances and thus made these points of weakness.

The majority of *lorica segmentata* components that have been found have been in obvious need of repair. That was, presumably, the reason they had been set aside and ultimately ended up deposited in the archaeological record: to be repaired, cannibalized or scrapped. Many of the finds also show signs of having already been repaired, typically manifested with fittings that do not match the original design or cruder riveting. Original rivets tended to have small, hemispherical heads, whereas repairs often featured non-matching, flat, asymmetrical heads, giving every sign of having been a hasty and (viewed with a mildly critical eye) inept, if functional, solution. Similarly, the detailed cutting that was necessary to form the fittings, when executed by skilled craftsmen, was a long way from the frankly inept and misshapen examples that have been found at some sites. Some fittings clearly originated with other, 'donor' cuirasses, which is one of the possible explanations for the armour that was found among the contents of the chest containing the Corbridge Hoard, since one of the type B/C upper sets seems to have been caught in the process of having its upper shoulderguard assembly removed and added to one of the type A shoulder sets which lacked such plates (Allason-Jones & Bishop 1988: 100). This was cannibalization in action, sacrificing components from a damaged cuirass to keep another one fit for service; armies have always done this and probably always will. The Roman fort in post-Boudican London produced more evidence of cannibalization, with an articulated set of *lorica segmentata* shoulder and collar plates, one component of which was missing (presumably removed), the remainder having been discarded as if of no further use. One of the valuable products of the discovery of the Corbridge Hoard is the revelation that Roman soldiers did not seem to have cared about the look of such repairs, which serves to

G **REPAIRING ARMOUR AT LEÓN**

The scene is a rectangular rampart-back building behind the southern defences of the legionary fortress at León in Hispania. The original 1st-century AD stone wall has been strengthened and raised by the addition of a new wall in front of (and incorporating) it and this can be seen above the original wall.

Through large, full-height openings with shutters pulled back, craftsman are hard at work repairing both Newstead and Corbridge types of *lorica segmentata*, as well as segmental armguards. In some cases, this involves taking one of the quarter-units of the armour to pieces, de-riveting the internal leathers or the brass fittings in order to replace them. The craftsmen, specialists in their tasks, are assisted by semi-skilled workers detailed from century strength to perform tasks like cutting out sheet metal or leather, acting as strikers around the anvil, or just sweeping the workshop clean. There are also slaves present to assist with the running of the facility (carrying fuel or water and raw materials), along with civilian contractors carting in supplies.

Upper backplate of *lorica segmentata* from the Corbridge Hoard (with rosette washer under the leathering rivet) incorrectly overlapped by the middle backplate below it. (Photo © M.C. Bishop)

remind us that modern concepts of military 'uniformity' were not necessarily observed in the same way in antiquity.

Often, repairs did not require major replacements, but rather minor 'tweaks'. The substitution of a copper-alloy fitting was a common solution on *lorica segmentata*. The Corbridge Hoard sets of armour include examples of replaced lobate hinges, as well as a former hinged joint on an upper shoulderguard repaired by simply riveting the plates together (thereby coincidentally demonstrating that the hinged joints on upper shoulderguards were far from essential). On Newstead-type cuirasses, a common solution to problems with missing tie rings or damaged fasteners was to use a strip of copper alloy bent around a circular-sectioned former as a replacement; this was used instead of tie loops on the girth hoops from Newstead and Zugmantel, as well as on the vertical fastener from Eining.

Repairs were not just confined to the metal components, however. The leathering was vulnerable to mechanical damage from repeated movement, particularly from plates rubbing or even cutting worn straps; from being soaked (whether by rain or perspiration) and then dried; while the riveting points were inevitably going to be points of stress. One of the sets of backplates from the Corbridge Hoard had had the two parallel leathers replaced by one large patch, ironically anticipating Groller's leather-based reconstruction. Re-leathering would be far less obvious when one strap was simply replaced with a newer one, although the variety of mixed decorative washers on some sets of armour may be indicators of repairs in this way.

The possibility that some older forms of segmental cuirass were upgraded when new forms appeared should also be considered. There is, for example, a mid-collar plate from the excavations at Chichester which has the lobate hinges of the Corbridge type but the broader dimensions of the Kalkriese form (Thomas 2003: 122, Fig. 79, 15).

The fittings of *lorica segmentata* are among the most common finds of armour to come from Roman military sites. This raises the question of just how common its use was: was it ubiquitous from the 1st century AD onwards, as the finds seem to suggest, or does the fragility of these fittings skew the finds spectrum in favour of segmental and against mail and scale armour? There is no way of being certain, but the images on the Adamclisi metopes and on gravestones seem to imply that mail and scale might have been just as prevalent among legionaries as *lorica segmentata*. Trajan's Column has done its job too well.

Examination of the sets of armguards found in the Carlisle excavations revealed a great deal about the repairs that had been undertaken during their lifetimes and showed them to have been just as vulnerable as segmental body armour (Bishop in Howard-Davis 2009: 694–700). Since some of them used dissimilar rivets to attach the internal leathering to the plates, it was possible to identify one *manica* that had been formed by joining sections from two different units, one of them originally being provided with copper-alloy rivets, the other with iron examples. This joining of two different assemblies was also apparent from a realignment of the internal leathering regime. Other signs of repairs include multiple rivet holes (and even rivets) at one location, as well as a number of examples of plates simply riveted together so that they no longer articulated. Because the elbow was the only region that demanded flexion in the defence, this was at least feasible for the upper and lower arm.

Asking why so many repairs were necessary for both segmental limb and body armour prompts some interesting observations. Riveting together plates that were originally articulated (evidenced for *lorica segmentata* and *manica* components) hints at an element of haste in their repair, while cannibalization – using elements of one defence to repair another – is indicative of an urgent need that could not be met by the manufacture of new items. The fact that such repairs were necessary on items that had presumably entered the archaeological record because they had been put aside for repair only serves to underline the pressure under which the Roman Army sometimes found itself, the reasons for which will be examined next.

PLATE ARMOUR IN USE

Understanding how all Roman armour was used has been greatly aided by the plethora of reconstructions based on archaeological evidence that followed on from Robinson's pioneering work, although, as with all experimental archaeology, they can only ever show what was possible, not what actually happened. That said, the overall fragility of segmental body armour in comparison to mail seems beyond doubt, and the archaeological evidence clearly indicates that the evolution of segmental armour was guided by pragmatic responses to genuine problems that arose from its use. It is not for the modern commentator to decry *lorica segmentata* as a flawed form of defence when the Romans seemed quite happy to rely on it in battle for more than 300 years.

Copper-alloy figurine from a shrine at Versigny interpreted as depicting a *crupellarius* gladiator. (Photo © Musée Jeanne d'Aboville/La Fère)

Combat

Unsurprisingly, perhaps, no unequivocal accounts survive of plate armour being employed in combat by the Roman Army. There is, however, a rather interesting description of the uprising of Sacrovir (together with Florus) in Gaul in AD 21:

> His followers amounted to forty thousand; one-fifth armed on the legionary model; the rest with boar-spears, knives, and other implements of the hunting-field. To these he added a contingent of slaves, destined to be gladiators and encased in the continuous shell of iron usual in the country: the so-called *crupellarii* – who, if too weighty to inflict wounds, were impregnably fortified against receiving them. (Tacitus, *Ann.* 3.43)

A copper-alloy statuette from Versigny (France) has been identified as depicting one of these *crupellarii* (Picard 1980). If this is a correct identification, then it is significant in that it depicts overlapping plate armour similar to *lorica segmentata* with *manicae* and thigh guards. Once the Roman forces of G. Silius confronted the rebel forces, the legionaries adopted some ingenious solutions to deal with these *crupellarii*: '... in front, the iron-clad men offered a brief impediment, as their plating was proof against *pilum* and sword. However, the legionaries seized their axes and pickaxes (*dolabrae*) and hacked at armour and flesh as if demolishing a wall: others overturned the inert masses with poles or forks, and left them lying like corpses unable to get up again' (Tacitus, *Ann.* 3.46).

This was the first time that legionaries in the western empire had encountered a foe wearing plate armour and experienced its efficacy against their traditional armament: the *pilum* and short sword. This in turn provides an important insight into how formidable legionaries equipped with plate armour must have seemed to their opponents. Nevertheless, all armour is a compromise between protection and mobility, and legionary *lorica segmentata* only really offered such protection to the torso, leaving plenty of vulnerable areas exposed. The *crupellarii* sacrificed mobility for increased protection, as Tacitus makes clear, although his observation about felled gladiators unable to get up again may just be his idea of an amusing aside or a literary *topos*, as used elsewhere when armoured Sarmatian cavalrymen are brought down by Roman troops and unable to get up (Tacitus, *Histories* 1.79).

In fact, the bulk of the evidence for the use of plate armour in combat comes from archaeological remains of the artefacts themselves. It has been argued that one of the explanations for the ubiquity of segmental armour fragments in the archaeological record is related to its vulnerability to damage for whatever reason. Indeed, traces of damage are rife among surviving pieces of *lorica segmentata* and *manica*; some of it clearly is the result of combat while other examples may also originate with enemy action but lack obvious signs to confirm it. The best example of what is probably combat attrition is a damaged Corbridge type A *lorica segmentata* breastplate from London which sustained a penetrating blow at some point before deposition. The fact that it was most likely being worn at the time is indicated by the limited amount of overall distortion to the plate beyond the actual penetration damage. This suggests that the body of the wearer and any garments worn between his body and the armour plate were supporting the plate as it was struck.

Ergonomic design was key to *lorica segmentata*, because (unlike mail and scale) every care was taken to deflect blows in much the same way that it was with Roman helmets. The upper and lesser shoulderguards sought to deflect blows outwards and downwards in much the same way that the girth hoops did. Additionally, the upper shoulderguards served to provide additional shock absorption and reinforcement for the shoulder region, in much the same way as shoulder doubling in mail or scale cuirasses. This was partly as a result of the overlapping plates being supported on the internal leathering, but also one of the possible functions of the otherwise enigmatic hinges between plates: to introduce some 'give' and thereby dissipate the energy of a blow.

BELOW LEFT

Interior view of an over-compressed set of Corbridge type B/C girth hoops from the Corbridge Hoard with the remains of the internal leathers and the pairs of copper-alloy rivets attaching them to each ferrous strip. (Photo © M.C. Bishop)

BELOW RIGHT

A reconstructed set of Corbridge-type *lorica segmentata* girth hoops showing how they stand naturally on slightly worn internal leathers with a degree of sag and demonstrating how much they would have to be compressed to match the girth hoop sets in the Corbridge Hoard. (Photo © M.C. Bishop)

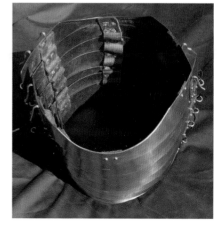

Re-enactors wearing Corbridge-type *loricae segmentatae* showing the same misaligned backplates evidenced by archaeological finds. (Photo © M.C. Bishop)

Carriage

One problem with Robinson's reconstruction of *lorica segmentata* was readily apparent from the way that it sat upon the human frame. There was an unavoidable 'sag' in the shoulder sections which caused the breastplates to overlap at an angle, producing an awkward gap between the breastplates, although the placement of the fastenings upon them implied that this should not in fact have been the case. Most suggestions to counter this problem, including the possibility that an additional 'centre plate' had somehow been missed (Daniels in Allason-Jones & Bishop 1988: 99), bore no fruit, but there was nevertheless a simple solution in both the ancient literary sources and in the study of medieval and post-medieval armour: padding. All armour required some sort of lining or undergarment, such as an arming doublet or aketon, to help spread the force of a blow against the carapace of the armour. Such garments seem to be described in both the Late Roman *De Rebus Militaris* by an unknown author, in which it was called the *thoracomachus* (Bishop 1995), and in a similarly anonymous Byzantine military manual (Dennis 1985: 55). It did not need to be particularly thick over most of the body to be effective, but such a garment offered the ideal place to incorporate some padding on the shoulders to counter the natural slope of the *trapezius* muscles which was causing the sag observed in reconstruction segmental cuirasses. Such a garment was also the obvious means of attaching the *pteryges* visible with muscled cuirasses and *lorica segmentata* and, indeed, examples occasionally appear in representational art, such as on a relief now in the Baths of Diocetian in Rome (Robinson 1975: Fig. 158). These strips, variously shown as both rigid and flexible, may have been formed from double-thickness tanned leather, which would have afforded some limited protection to those parts of the body left uncovered by armour, such as the tops of the shoulders or the buttocks and lower torso. The *pteryges* were usually in two overlapping layers and, when worn with the muscled cuirass, the top layer was sometimes folded over a waist belt, as with the officer depicted on the Louvre Praetorians relief. *Pteryges* can also be seen being

For storage or transport, segmental body armour could be disassembled into its four constituent components (two upper and two lower halves) and partially collapsed. Over-enthusiastic compression could, however, lead to damage to the internal leathering regime and potentially to the metal fittings too. It was in this form that the pieces of armour were found in the chest containing the Corbridge Hoard: crammed together to make them as small as possible. These Corbridge-type *lorica segmentata* girth hoops from Rißtissen demonstrate the same sort of over-compression found in the Corbridge Hoard, indicating that the set was forcibly compressed for storage. Examination of the mineral-preserved remains of the armour in the Corbridge Hoard revealed that it had been wrapped in cloth prior to deposition, presumably to help protect it. (Drawing © M.C. Bishop)

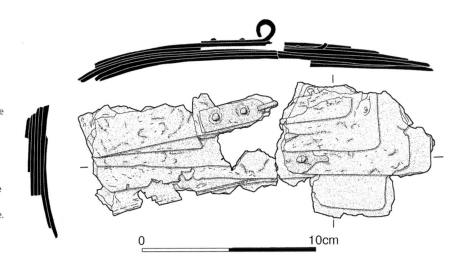

0   10cm

worn with 2nd-century segmental armour on the Marcus Column, on the panels of Marcus Aurelius on the Arch of Constantine, and on a copper-alloy figurine now in the British Museum in London.

The implication of using external vertical strap fasteners on the front of the Kalkriese and Corbridge type A cuirasses, but internal buckles at the rear, is that the cuirass was designed to be put on with the back fastened and the front unfastened, so that the wearer could put on and take off his own armour without the need for assistance.

It is difficult to believe that that Corbridge Hoard contained three left and three right upper units (two A, one B/C in each case), as well as the same number (and type) of lower units. This would imply – if indeed these were deposited as complete sets – that the Romans were not overly fussy about whether cuirass halves matched perfectly; and, ignoring typological niceties, that there may have been both B and C fittings together on the same cuirass!

Versatility

A key advantage to *lorica segmentata* was that it allowed for the full six degrees of freedom in bodily movement. It was by no means the only form of armour to do this (mail was just as flexible, although heavier), but this meant that it was possible to march, work and fight while wearing the cuirass. The sculptors on the helical frieze of Trajan's Column showed citizen troops performing all of these tasks, including the construction of fortifications, while wearing segmental body armour. A detail on that frieze (Scene XXVI) depicts a legionary wading across a river. His body armour, which is very clearly *lorica segmentata*, is resting in the hollow of his shield, which he holds above his head (Bishop 2020: 58 Fig.). Although these are all extremely enticing images, it is unclear to what extent they represent artistic licence on

 SEGMENTATA STORED AT CARNUNTUM

The *armamentarium* built into the rampart immediately behind the western wall of the legionary fortress at Carnuntum near Bad Deutsch-Altenburg was found to contain a wide range of weaponry when it was excavated. In this reconstruction, two different types of *lorica segmentata* – Corbridge and Newstead – can be seen in various states of disassembly on the sets of shelves where they have been stored. In the background, other types of armour can be seen stored on shelves, including mail and scale cuirasses. There are also intact armguards hanging from the shelves, as well as components from such defences once again awaiting repair or cannibalization.

the part of the metropolitan sculptors as opposed to observation of actual practices undertaken by troops in the field. Indeed, the notion that the scenes shown on the reliefs were based on accurate 'field sketches' has been called into question in recent years.

Segmentata was lighter than scale or mail – reconstructions typically weigh between 5kg and 9kg – which meant it was less fatiguing to wear, and arguably offered better protection than the other two main types of body armour in certain circumstances. Other advantages include its diminished requirements for raw materials, its ease of manufacture and the time taken to manufacture it (Sim & Kaminiski 2012: 137–38). Since the Roman state was mining the raw materials, harvesting scrap for re-use or re-forging, and fabricating and mending the armour, the cost was in terms of time and manpower, rather than money. This is why the haste of some repairs (see p.52) is significant.

Who wore what?

If nothing else, the overly simplified categories of troops represented on Trajan's Column should warn against using the sculptures of that monument as a literal representation of what the various components of the Roman Army may have looked like. Segmental cuirasses were reserved for citizen troops belonging to the Praetorian Guard or the legions. This is confirmed by the Adamclisi metopes, on which citizen soldiers are only shown wearing mail or scale cuirasses.

Archaeological evidence has been used to try to counter the impression given by the reliefs of Trajan's Column and suggest that it was not just legionary infantry who used *lorica segmentata*. Fittings are known from a number of smaller Roman military sites from the early Principate of a type unlike the fortresses large enough to accommodate one or more legions. Although inscriptions do not survive from early timber forts, it has been argued by analogy with later installations that demonstrably held auxiliary troops, such as those along Hadrian's Wall, that it must also have been the case for these earlier sites. As a hypothesis, this is crucially flawed, because legionary detachments are well known to have been outposted in smaller forts (e.g. Tacitus, *Ann*. 3.74).

Additionally, forts have produced this material in the province of Raetia (now part of modern-day Germany) which initially had no legion as part of its forces. Some scholars have concluded that here auxiliaries also used the *lorica segmentata*. The discovery of a helmet in the river near the Roman fortlet of Burlafingen seriously undermines this interpretation, however, since it bore the ownership inscription of a soldier in *legio XVI Gallica*, thought to have been based at Mainz in Germania Superior, at the time of the loss of the helmet. In reality, legions based in provinces under commanders appointed by the emperor frequently deployed into neighbouring provinces as required by circumstance. This also happened more than once with Judaea, well before the Jewish uprising of AD 66–70. There is thus no reason why legionary equipment – in this case *lorica segmentata* – should not be found in provinces without a permanent legionary establishment.

So it seems that Trajan's Column may in some respects have been correct in attributing segmental body armour to legionaries and praetorians, but this has to be qualified by noting that there is substantial evidence (both sculptural and archaeological) that these troops *also* used scale and mail armour. In other words, the sculptors of Trajan's Column were deliberately selective in their decision to indicate citizen troops by means of *lorica segmentata*, together with shield types and military standards.

Legacy

Segmental plate armour was known long before the Romans – the set of Mycenaean bronze armour from Dendra (Greece) comes to mind – and it was of course widely utilized in the medieval and post-medieval period. There is no need to seek a connection between these instances, however. Articulated plate armour was such an obvious solution to enhanced bodily protection for soldiers that it is unsurprising that it was invented more than once. The lack of scholarly interest in Trajan's Column and similar monuments before the Renaissance ensured that articulated medieval plate armour – even those with sliding rivets – owed nothing to the Romans.

The absence of a direct line of transmission of the idea of segmental armour does not mean that Roman *lorica segmentata* was not influential. That legacy was artistic, however, and not military. From the earliest sketches made of Trajan's Column, via Hollywood epics, to the latest television dramas, the identification of Roman soldiers with this type of armour is absolute and the two are difficult to prise apart. Whether depicting the Republican period, the Principate or the Dominate, Spartacus or Constantine, Hollywood and the visual media have frequently reverted to that agenda set by Trajan's Column, so effective has it been at transmitting its message.

The love of classical imagery so typical of Renaissance art has also meant that the individual, heroic officer or emperor in a muscled cuirass has become just as powerful an image as the massed ranks of *segmentata*-clad legionaries shuffling across the silver screen. A statue of King James II in Trafalgar Square in London is a perfect example of the adoption of this persona in comparatively recent history: wearing an elaborately decorated muscled cuirass (rather confusingly rendered with a scale texture) adorned with *pteryges* at both the arms and waist, he is the epitome of what has recently come to be known as 'classical reception'. Similarly, the figurehead of the Royal Yacht HMS *Royal George* depicting King George IV in a Roman cuirass (now in the collection of the National Maritime Museum in Greenwich, London) continued this tradition into the 19th century.

The popularity of Roman re-enactment and living history in general have guaranteed that Henry Russell Robinson's legacy, as the person who (along with Charles Daniels) pieced together and began to understand the original find of cuirasses from Corbridge, before going on to produce his own fully functional replicas, would enhance (if not replace) the original first examinations of Trajan's Column. Today, Roman re-enactment groups are numerous and worldwide, but the armour they wear owes more to Robinson than it does to Trajan's Column. Some re-enactors make their own cuirasses, but many buy from commercial vendors (often producing the components on the Indian subcontinent, using the workshop skills of the craftsmen there). This in turn means that it is now possible to buy a more-or-less accurate set of *lorica segmentata* online, so the legacy of this form of plate armour is assured.

Copper-alloy figurine of a legionary wearing *lorica segmentata*, now in the British Museum (acquired from the collection of Alessandro Castellani in 1867). The style of beard suggests that it dates to the latter half of the 2nd century AD. (© The Trustees of the British Museum)

BIBLIOGRAPHY

Ancient sources

AE – *L'Année Epigraphique*. Available from Epigraphik-Datenbank Clauss/Slaby at https://tinyurl.com/ryexz6k

Arrian, *Techne Taktike*, eds R. Hercher and A. Eberhard. Available at https://tinyurl.com/vkn8fmbt

CIL – *Corpus Inscriptionum Latinarum*. Epigraphik-Datenbank Clauss/Slaby. Available at https://tinyurl.com/ryexz6k

Justinian, *Digest*. 1932 Central Trust Company edition, trans. S.P. Scott. Available at https://tinyurl.com/ybc66j2j

Livy, *History of Rome*. 1912, trans. Revd Canon Roberts. Available at https://tinyurl.com/wnnnm7k

Notitia Dignitatum. Available at https://tinyurl.com/uvz3z4e

Pliny the Elder, *Natural History*. 1855–57 Bohn edition, trans. J. Bostock & H.T. Riley. Available at https://tinyurl.com/cvmp3bu

Polybios, *Histories*. 1922–27 Loeb edition, trans. W.R. Paton. Available at https://tinyurl.com/298bsf

RIB – *Roman Inscriptions of Britain*. Available at https://tinyurl.com/rmxz8q9

Tab. Vind. – Tabulae Vindolandenses. Available from Vindolanda Tablets Online at https://tinyurl.com/m7gnl5

Tacitus, *Agricola*. 1876, trans. A.J. Church & W.J. Brodribb. Available at https://tinyurl.com/v2oqbvp

Tacitus, *Annals and Histories*. 1925–37 Loeb edition, trans. J. Jackson. Available at https://tinyurl.com/8jpv49

Varro, *On the Latin Language*. 1938 Loeb edition, trans. R.G. Kent. Available at https://tinyurl.com/rhade6v

Vegetius, *De Re Militari*. 1885 Lang. Available at https://tinyurl.com/ybvq5ypu

Modern sources

Allason-Jones, L. and Bishop, M.C. (1988). *Excavations at Roman Corbridge: the Hoard*, HBMCE Archaeological Report No. 7. London: English Heritage.

Aurrecoechea, J. (2003/04). 'New perspectives on the evolution and chronology of Roman segmental armour (*lorica segmentata* and *manica*), based on Hispanic finds', *JRMES* 14/15: 49–55.

Aurrecoechea, J., Fernández Ibáñez, C., García Marcos, V. & Morillo, Á. (2008). 'Un protector laminado de brazo (manica) procedente del campamento de la Legio VII Gemina en León', *Archivo Español de Arqueología* 81: 255–64.

Aurrecoechea, J. & Muñoz Villarejo, F. (2001/02). 'A legionary workshop of the 3rd century AD specialising in *loricae segmentatae* from the Roman fortress in León (Spain)', *JRMES* 12/13: 15–28.

Băeştean, G. & Barbu, M. (2015). 'Ulpia Traiana Sarmizegetusa. About the wooden phase structures on the *Insula 3*', *Sargetia. Acta Musei Devensis* (S.N.) 6: 181–92.

Bergemann, J. (1990). *Römische Reiterstatuen. Ehrendenkmäler im öffentlichen Bereich*. Mainz: von Zabern.

Bishop, M.C. (1995). 'Aketon, *thoracomachus*, and *lorica segmentata*', *Exercitus* 3:1: 1–3.

Bishop, M.C. (2002). *Lorica Segmentata I. A Handbook of Articulated Roman Plate Armour*, JRMES Monograph 1. Chirnside: The Armatura Press.

Bishop, M.C. (2015). 'The Eining *lorica segmentata*', in P. Henrich, Ch. Miks, J. Obmann & M. Wieland, eds, *NON SOLUM ... SED ETIAM. Festschrift für Thomas Fischer zum 65. Geburtstag*. Rahden: Leidorf: pp. 31–40.

Bishop, M.C. (2016). *The Gladius: The Roman Short Sword*. Weapon 51. Oxford: Osprey Publishing.

Bishop, M.C. (2020). *Roman Shields*. Elite 234. Oxford: Osprey Publishing.

Bishop, M.C. & Coulston, J.C.N. (2006). *Roman Military Equipment from the Punic Wars to the Fall of Rome*, 2nd Edition. Oxford: Oxbow Books.

Brüggler, M., Dirsch, C., Drechsler, M., Schwab, R. & Willer, F. (2012). 'Ein römischer Schienenarmschutzaus dem Auxiliarlager Till-Steincheshof und die Messingherstellung in der römischen Kaiserzeit', *Bonner Jahrbücher* 212: 121–52.

Burns, M. (2005). *The Cultural and Military Significance of the South Italic Warrior's Panoply from the 5th to the 3rd Centuries BC.* Unpublished PhD thesis, University College London. Available at https://core.ac.uk/display/78075788 (accessed 27.6.21).

Caruana, I. (1993). 'A third-century *lorica segmentata* back-plate from Carlisle', *Arma* 5: 15–18.

Crossland, D. (2020). Oldest Roman body armour discovered in Germany, *The Times* 26.9.20. Available at https://www.thetimes.co.uk/article/oldest-roman-body-armour-discovered-in-germany-p6lsv5jq6 (accessed 15.6.21).

Curle, J. (1911). *A Roman Frontier Post and its People. The Fort at Newstead.* Glasgow: Maclehose.

Dennis, G.T. (1985). *Three Byzantine Military Treatises.* Washington, DC: Dumbarton Oaks, Research Library and Collection.

Dobson, C. (2018). *As Tough as Old Boots: Essays on the Manufacture and History of Hardened-Leather Armour.* Florence: Dobson.

Gabelmann, H. (1973). 'Römische Grabmonumente mit Reiterkampfszenen in Rheingebiet', *Bonner Jahrbücher* 173: 132–200.

Garbsch, J. (1978). *Römische Paraderüstungen.* Munich: Beck.

Groller, M. von (1901). 'Römische Waffen', *Der Römischer Limes in Österreich* 2: 85–132.

Howard-Davis, C. (2009). *The Carlisle Millennium Project: Excavations in Carlisle, 1998–2001, Volume 2,* Lancaster imprints 15, Lancaster: Oxford Archaeology North.

Lipsius, J. (1630). *De Militia Romana Libri Quinque, Commentarius Ad Polybium.* Antwerp: Officina Plantiniana.

McNally, M. (2011). *Teutoburg Forest AD 9: The destruction of Varus and his legions.* Campaign 228. Oxford: Osprey.

Mutz, A. (1987). 'Die Deutung eines Eisenfundes aus dem spätrepublikanischen Legionslager Cáceres el Viejo (Spanien)', *Jahresberichte aus Augst und Kaiseraugst* 7: 323–30.

Picard, G.C. (1980). 'Cruppellarii', in H. Le Bonniec and G. Vallet (eds), *Mélanges de littérature et d'épigraphie latines, d'histoire ancienne et d'archéologie. Hommages à la mémoire de Pierre Wuilleumier.* Paris: Les Belles Lettres: pp. 277–80.

Robinson, H.R. (1974). 'Problems in reconstructing Roman armour', in E. Birley, B. Dobson & M.G. Jarrett, eds, *Roman Frontier Studies 1969.* Cardiff: University of Wales: pp. 24–35.

Robinson, H.R. (1975). *The Armour of Imperial Rome.* London: Arms & Armour Press.

Sim, D. & Kaminski, J. (2012). *Roman Imperial Armour: The Production of Early Imperial Military Armour.* Oxford: Oxbow Books.

Stemmer, K. (1978). *Untersuchungen zur Typologie, Chronologie und Ikonographie der Panzerstatuen.* Berlin: Mann.

Stiebel, G.D. (2014). 'Military equipment', in Syon, D., *Gamla III. The Shmarya Gutmann Excavations 1976–1989. Finds and Studies, Part 1.* IAA Reports 56. Jerusalem: IAA: pp. 57–107.

Syon, D. (2014). *Gamla III. The Shmarya Gutmann Excavations 1976–1989. Finds and Studies, Part 1.* IAA Reports 56. Jerusalem: IAA.

Thomas, M.D. (2003). *Lorica Segmentata II. A Catalogue of Finds.* JRMES Monograph 2. Chirnside: The Armatura Press.

Webster, G. (1960). 'A note on the Roman cuirass (*lorica segmentata*)', *Journal of the Arms and Armour Society* 3: 194–97.

Weinberg, S.S. (1979). 'A hoard of Roman armor', *Antike Kunst* 22: 82–86.

0   10cm

Copper-alloy armguard, still articulated, excavated from the auxiliary fort at Till-Steincheshof and dating to the 2nd century AD. (Drawing © M.C. Bishop)

INDEX

References to illustrations are shown in
bold. Plates are shown with page locators in
parentheses.